Burke's Speech

on

Conciliation with America

Edited, with Introduction and Notes, by

F. G. Selby

M.A. Oxon., Hon. LL.D. Bombay

LONDON
MACMILLAN & CO LTD
NEW YORK · ST MARTIN'S PRESS
1964

*First Edition 1912
Reprinted 1917, 1918, 1919, 1934, 1949, 1953
1955, 1956, 1961, 1964*

MACMILLAN AND COMPANY LIMITED
*St Martin's Street London WC 2
also Bombay Calcutta Madras Melbourne*

THE MACMILLAN COMPANY OF CANADA LIMITED
70 Bond Street Toronto 2

ST MARTIN'S PRESS INC
175 Fifth Avenue New York 10 NY

PRINTED IN GREAT BRITAIN

CONTENTS

INTRODUCTION

EDMUND BURKE was born at Dublin, at the end of 1728
or the beginning of 1729. He was first returned to Parliament, as member for the borough of Wendover, at
the end of 1765, the year in which George Grenville,
the author of the Stamp Act, was dismissed from office.
Grenville was succeeded by Lord Rockingham, the head
of a party which Burke regarded as the most honest
and patriotic party in the country, and which he was
largely instrumental in keeping together. Rockingham,
by whom the Stamp Act was repealed, remained in
office for one year and twenty days. After him came
the Chatham ministry. Before the end of the year
Chatham's health broke down. The Duke of Grafton
then led the ministry, and after him Lord North, who
remained at the head of affairs for twelve years, from
1770-1782. The opening years of the reign of George
III. were years of disturbance and difficulty. The ele-
vation of Bute to the premiership, after the disgrace of
Pitt and the dismissal of Newcastle, had produced a
violent prejudice against the Scotch. Then came the
troubles with America. There was, besides, the excitement caused by the affair of Wilkes. It seemed likely

that the majority of the House of Commons would
arrogate to itself the right of determining whom the
constituencies might elect to sit as their representatives.
There were violent riots in London, provoked by the
sympathy of the mob with Wilkes, and by general
detestation of the arbitrary conduct of the House of
Commons. Burke's view of the period, his explanation
of the disorders, and the remedies which he proposed,
are set forth in his pamphlet on *The Cause of the Present
Discontents*, published in 1770.

Burke sat in the Parliament of 1774 as member for
Bristol, of which city he continued to be the representative for six years. He made himself unpopular with
his constituents by the support which he gave to the
abolition of restrictions on Irish trade, and to the removal of unreasonable disabilities on Catholics. In this
year he made his speech on American taxation, and in
1775 the speech on Conciliation with America. In 1777
appeared his Letter to the Sheriffs of Bristol on the
affairs of America. In 1780 matters were complicated
at home by the anti-popery Gordon riots. Burke was
endangered because he, as a Whig, had advocated a
milder treatment of Catholics. It was in this year that
he presented to the House his scheme of Economic Reform. His object was to abolish all the lucrative sine-
cures, by means of which the Court could corrupt the
House of Commons, and turn it into a mere tool of
despotism. This was Burke's substitute for those
schemes of organic reform which he always opposed.
In this year he lost his seat for Bristol, but was returned as member for the borough of Malton. When
Lord North's government came to an end in 1782, the

Rockingham party again came into power. Notwithstanding the services which Burke had rendered to the
party, he was not admitted into the Cabinet. Lord
Rockingham died after three months of office. The
Ministry was split up. Some of them supported the
claims of Shelburne, others those of Fox, who was now
the head of the Rockingham section of the Whigs, to
the vacant premiership. The king preferred Shelburne.
It was unfortunate that the whole Whig party could not
act together. We must regret that Burke rendered the
party powerless by aiding to split it into two halves,
and that he offered a violent and factious opposition to
the Ministry. The Shelburne administration fell in the
spring of 1783, and Fox and Burke, to their disgrace,
went over to their old enemy Lord North. A Coalition
Ministry was formed, but was dismissed in December,
1783, on the rejection of Fox's India Bill. Pitt was
made prime minister, and the power of the Whigs was
at an end for half a century. Burke began by opposing
ɩ measure brought forward by Pitt, which was practically
a proposal to give to Ireland complete commercial freedom, on condition that she paid a contribution from her
surplus revenue to the Imperial Treasury. Lord Morley
points out that Burke's conduct can only be justified
on the ground that Pitt's proposals "amounted to an
attempt to extract revenue from Ireland, identical in
purpose, principle, and probable effect with the ever me-
morable attempt to extract revenue from the American
colonies." In 1787 he opposed Pitt's proposed treaty of
commerce with France, "which enabled the subjects of
both countries to reside and travel in either without
license or passport, did away with all prohibitions of

trade on either side, and reduced every import duty." [1]
But, so far as Burke was concerned, the most remarkable
event of the session was, of course, the impeachment of
Warren Hastings. He opened the case in 1788, and the
verdict was delivered in 1795. To the affairs of India,
generally, Burke really devoted the labour of fourteen
years, from 1781 to 1795. Burke next opposed Pitt's
Regency Bill, the principle of which was that the Prince
of Wales could not claim to act as Regent, but that it
lay with the Parliament to appoint the Regent and to
define the terms on which he held office. During this
period, Burke appears, by his unreasonableness, to have
lost his influence in the country, and the confidence of
his party and his friends. But with the French Revolution all this was changed. On this subject he was at
variance with Fox from the first. In 1790 he supported
the bill for the increase of the English army, and he
took occasion to declare that he would not remain on
terms of friendship with any one who should in any way
further the introduction of a democracy like that of
France. Fox expressed in the House his high sense of
the value of Burke's friendship. When Sheridan dis-
sented from the views expressed in Burke's speech,
Burke openly broke with him. In the same year, when
Fox proposed, what Burke had before advocated, namely,
a repeal of the Test and Corporation Act, Burke turned
round and opposed it, declaring that Dissenters were
disaffected citizens. It was in November, 1790, that he
published his *Reflections on the Revolution in France.* It
was hailed with delight by the Crown and the Tories.
In 1791 Burke openly broke with Fox on the subject of

[1] Green's *Short History of the English People*, p. 772.

the French Revolution. In August of the same year he published his *Appeal from the New to the Old Whigs*, in which he explained and defended his views on the French Revolution, and vindicated himself against the charge of having abandoned, in his criticisms on that event, the Whig principles which he had professed through life. A few months after the publication of the *Reflections*, he had issued his *Letter to a Member of the National Assembly*, which was full of violent abuse of the Revolution and its authors. In the same letter he hinted that a European intervention in favour of the French king might become necessary. By the end of the year 1791 he had himself become convinced that it was necessary. Henceforth he devoted himself to the advocacy of war against the French, and of repressive measures at home to stop the spread of Jacobin opinions. It was the murder of the French king which roused opinion in England to sympathy with Burke. In 1794 he retired from Parliament. Arrangements were being made for creating him a peer, but, in August of that year, he was completely broken by the death of his son. The question of the peerage was dropped, and a pension was granted to him. His *Letter to a Noble Lord* is a vindication, at once spirited and pathetic, of his right to a pension on the score of his political services. In 1795 he wrote the *Letters on a Regicide Peace*, which are, like the rest of his writings on the subject, characterized by violent hatred of all that was being done in France. The death of his son threw a profound melancholy over his closing years, and he died July 9th, 1797.

"Of all Burke's writings none are so fit to receive unqualified and unanimous admiration as the speech on

American taxation, the speech on Conciliation with America, and the Letter to the Sheriffs of Bristol. It is no exaggeration to say that they compose the most perfect manual in our literature, or in any literature, for one who approaches the study of public affairs, whether for knowledge or practice. They are an example without fault of all the qualities which the critic, whether a theorist or an actor, of great political situations should strive, by night and by day, to possess. If the theme with which they deal were less near than it is to our interests and affections as free citizens, these three performances would still abound in the lessons of an incomparable political method. . . . we should still have everything to learn from the author's treatment; the vigorous grasp of masses of compressed detail, the wide illumination from great principles of human experience, the strong and masculine feeling for the two great political ends of Justice and Freedom, the large and generous interpretation of expediency, the morality, the vision, the noble temper." [1]

The more carefully the pieces mentioned by Lord Morley are studied, the truer does his verdict appear. A teacher can do little more than repeat to his pupils the advice of Fox, " to read the speech on Conciliation by day, and meditate upon it by night : to peruse it again and again, study it, imprint it on their minds, and impress it upon their hearts." He who will do this will be rewarded by attaining ' large and liberal ideas in politics.'

It is not necessary to go minutely into contemporary politics to appreciate these writings. I have not

[1] Lord Morley.

attempted more in this Introduction than to give just
so much information as is necessary to enable the reader
to understand Burke. It is characteristic of Burke that
the permanent value of his work is independent of the
rightness or wrongness of his judgment on a particular
question. The value of a set of principles is not affected
by an erroneous application of them. Even those, therefore, who disagree with Burke's American policy have
everything to learn from his American speeches and
writings. Burke did not really understand the French
Revolution, but his Reflections on it have a universal
and permanent value as a philosophical vindication of
society, and an exposition of the eternal conditions of
order. We go to Burke not so much for a history of
a particular crisis, as to learn how to approach and treat
political questions. Nowhere is his political method
more clearly explained than in his American writings.
Nowhere are the obligations of an Imperial power, and
the great principles which should control Imperial
policy, more luminously set forth. One explanation then
of Burke's lasting fame is this, that he always rises above
the particular incidents treated of, to the explanation of
them, and that he teaches those who will listen to him
to rise above the disturbing influences of private interests and passions, and to judge events and regulate
conduct calmly and dispassionately, from the point of
view of prudence and morality.

Another circumstance which places Burke high in the
esteem of philosophical students of politics is this, that
in his writings is to be found a treatment of many forms
of government. In the British constitution he saw 'a
nice equipoise' of monarchical, aristocratic, and demo-

cratic elements : and he believed that the safety of
English liberties depended on the preservation of that
equipoise. When he saw any one of these elements
unduly encroaching on the rest, he came to the rescue
of the weaker parts. So that, if we study his writings
through, we find an appreciation of all these elements, and
a determination of their proper limits. The pamphlet
on *the Present Discontents* points out the danger of an
absolute Crown and Court, and advocates what we
should call 'liberal' principles. In the *Reflections on the
French Revolution,* on the other hand, we find an appreciation of the merits of aristocracy and of monarchy.

Then, again, Burke influences by his language. In
other speeches and writings we find examples of the
most gorgeous rhetoric, of extravagant declamation, of
fierce denunciation. The speech printed in this volume
is a model of calm persuasive argumentation. There are
passages of striking eloquence, such as the description of
the American fisheries, but they are introduced naturally
and without effort. They are called forth by the subject
and the feelings which it necessarily excites. But, taking
the speech as a whole, the reader cannot fail to be struck
by the skill with which Burke gives to his arguments the
air of truisms, and to his policy the air of common sense.
He wants, not to threaten or to ridicule, but to conciliate
and to persuade. It is not meant by this that he is dull
or trite. Common sense, as applied to Burke, does not
mean commonplace. The speech, like all that he said
or wrote, is conspicuous for grasp of the subject, for
knowledge of human nature, for far-sighted prudence,
and wide experience. It was, indeed, owing precisely
to those qualities which have given to the productions

of Burke a permanent value, and won for them a lasting
admiration, that they failed to produce an effect upon
the audience to which they were addressed.

For Englishmen, at any rate, the speeches and writings
of Burke derive an added interest from the patriotism
which inspires them. His fears for England called forth
the *Reflections on the Revolution in France*. They explain
his deep concern in the American question. In this
connection, the following passage from his *Address to the
King*[1] deserves careful study :—" It is not, Sire, from a
want of the most inviolable duty to your Majesty, not
from a want of a partial and a passionate regard to that
part of your Empire in which we reside, and which we
wish to be supreme, that we have hitherto withstood all
attempts to render the supremacy of one part of your
dominions inconsistent with the liberty and safety of
all the rest. The motives of our opposition are found in
those very sentiments which we are supposed to
violate. For we are convinced beyond a doubt that a
system of dependence, which leaves no security to the
people for any part of their freedom in their own hands,
cannot be established in any inferior member of the
British Empire, without consequentially destroying the
freedom of that very body, in favour of whose boundless
pretensions such a scheme is adopted. We know and
feel that arbitrary power over distant regions is not
within the competence, nor to be exercised agreeably
to the forms, or consistently with the spirit, of great
popular assemblies. If such assemblies are called to a
nominal share in the exercise of such power, in order to
screen, under a general participation, the guilt of des-

[1] Published in vol. v. of Bohn's edition of Burke's Works.

perate measures, it tends only the more deeply to corrupt
the deliberative character of those assemblies, in training
them to blind obedience, in habituating them to proceed
upon grounds of fact, with which they can rarely be
sufficiently acquainted, and in rendering them executive
instruments of designs, the bottom of which they cannot
possibly fathom.

To leave any real freedom to Parliament, freedom
must be left to the Colonies. A military government is
the only substitute for civil liberty. That the establishment of such a power in America will utterly ruin our
finances (though its certain effect) is the smallest part
of our concern. It will become an apt, powerful, and
certain engine for the destruction of our freedom here.
Great bodies of armed men, trained to a contempt
of popular assemblies representative of an English
people : kept up for the purpose of exacting impositions
without their consent, and maintained by that exaction ;
instruments in subverting, without any process of law,
great ancient establishments and respected forms of
governments ; set free from, and therefore above, the
ordinary English tribunals of the country where they
serve ;—these men cannot so transform themselves,
merely by crossing the sea, as to behold with love and
reverence, and submit with profound obedience to the
very same things in Great Britain which in America they
had been taught to despise, and had been accustomed to
awe and humble. All your Majesty's troops, in the
rotation of service, will pass through this discipline, and
contract these habits. If we could flatter ourselves that
this would not happen, we must be the weakest of men :
we must be the worst, if we were indifferent whether it

happened or not. What, gracious sovereign, is the Empire of America to us, or the Empire of the world, if we lose our own liberties? We deprecate this last of evils— we deprecate the effect of the doctrines which must support and countenance the government over conquered Englishmen."

The four Colonies constituting New England, namely, Massachusetts, New Hampshire, Connecticut, and Rhode Island, owed their origin to the Puritans, the first of whom went over in the *May Flower* in 1620. New York was first colonized by the Dutch at the beginning of the 17th century. It was ceded by them to Charles II., who granted it to his brother the Duke of York, from whom it derives its present name. It was originally called New Amsterdam. New Jersey, which, at first, formed part of the Dutch settlement, was separated from it by the Duke of York, and sold to Lord Berkeley and Sir George Carteret. The name was given in honour of Carteret's defence of the island of Jersey against the forces of the Long Parliament. Lord Berkeley sold his share to an association of Quakers, and the district was divided between them and Carteret. Under Queen Anne the heirs of Carteret surrendered their rights to the Crown, and the two districts were reunited under one government. The plural name Jerseys was, however, still retained. Pennsylvania was opened out by the Quaker Penn, who in 1681 obtained from the Crown a grant of forest (*sylvan*) land beyond the river Delaware. The State of Delaware was in some measure dependent on Pennsylvania. It passed from Dutch to English hands along with New York. The name is derived from an Englishman who

was Captain General of Virginia in the time of James I.
Maryland was named after the Queen of Charles I., who
made Lord Baltimore proprietary of the territory. His
name is preserved in that of the capital of the state.
Virginia, the earliest of the chartered colonies, was
named in honour of Queen Elizabeth. But it was not
really settled until the time of James I. The rights of
the company to which it was assigned passed to the
Crown in 1624. The territory of North and South
Carolina was granted by charter to a number of pro-
prietaries by Charles II. in 1663. Their rights reverted
to the Crown in 1729. Georgia, named after George
II., was established by some philanthropic Englishmen
who obtained a charter from the Crown in 1732.

At the time when the troubles with England began,
the population of these thirteen colonies was about two
millions of European blood, and half a million of others.
In each Colony there was an elected Assembly, a Council, sometimes nominated, sometimes elected, and a
Governor nominated by the Crown, or when there
were proprietors, by them jointly with the Crown.
In Connecticut and Rhode Island alone the Governor
was elected.

Grenville conceived the idea of raising revenue in
America on the ground that the Americans should
help to defray the expenses of the Seven Years' War,
which had been undertaken partly in their defence.
His suggestion in 1764 to raise money by a Stamp
Duty, or by any other duty which the colonists might
prefer, reached them just when they were suffering
from a war with the Indians on their frontiers, and
when they were irritated by measures which England

had recently taken to deprive them of the profits of their large contraband trade. They were still further irritated by certain extra duties which Grenville had just levied on their foreign imports, though they did not deny the right of Parliament to levy duties of that kind.

To Grenville's suggestion they replied that they would not accept the Stamp Duty or any alternative to it, on the ground that they could not lawfully be taxed by a House of Commons in which they were not represented. If they granted any supplies, it would only be through a vote of their own Assemblies, on a requisition made by the Crown through the Secretary of State. In the session of 1765 Grenville simply proposed to levy the Stamp Duties in America, hinting at the same time that this was only a first instalment of the revenue which he proposed to raise in that country. The Bill was passed almost without opposition, the House even refusing to look at petitions and remonstrances which some of the Colonies had addressed to it.

When the news of the passing of the Act reached America, Virginia set the example to the other Colonies of addressing remonstrances and petitions for repeal through the Assemblies to the Crown. At the same time, the necessity of joint action being felt, several Assemblies deputed delegates to a joint congress to be held in October, a month before the Stamp Act was to come into force. Delegates from nine Assemblies met together. Resolutions were passed denying the right of Parliament to tax America, and petitions to the King and the Parliament were agreed upon. Associations were also formed for discouraging the importation and use of British manufactures until the

Stamp Act should be repealed. In Boston there were serious riots.

When the first of November came it was found practically impossible to administer the Act, either because the people would not allow the stamped papers to be landed, or because those who had been appointed to distribute the papers resigned their posts when the time came. The Rockingham Ministry, who had not favoured the Stamp Act, were perplexed equally by the difficulty of enforcing it and by the dangerous precedent of conceding a repeal. There was an important debate when Parliament met in January, 1766. Pitt urged that the right to legislate did not include the right to tax, and he denied that the Americans were in any sense represented in the House of Commons. In reply, Grenville quoted precedents to show that taxation and representation had not always or necessarily gone together, and he said that the seditious spirit of the Colonies was encouraged by factions in the House. In reply, Pitt deprecated an appeal to obscure precedents in such a case. He lauded the spirit which the Americans had shown in resisting the Act, and argued that a victory over America in such a cause would be fatal to constitutional liberty in England. He advised that England's unlimited power of legislating for America should be affirmed, but that her right to tax should be denied, and that the Stamp Act should be immediately and totally repealed. Certain correspondence with America was then laid before the House, as were also petitions from the merchants of large towns in England praying for a repeal of the Act, on the ground that the interruption of American trade, due to the disturbances caused by it, would be the ruin of English merchants. At the same time the evidence of Franklin and other Americans was taken at the bar of the House as to the determination of the Americans to resist such taxation, and to abstain from the use of English goods until it was abandoned. After this interval proposals in accordance with Pitt's speech were laid before the House. It was found impossible to maintain the distinction between legislation and taxation, and an Act Declaratory of the absolute sovereignty of England over the Colonies was passed. But the proposal to repeal the Stamp Act met with a resolute opposition from the leaders of the late Administration, from many country gentlemen, who feared that concession to violence would constitute a dangerous precedent, and from the King's friends.

Conway, on behalf of the Government, asked leave to bring in a bill for the repeal of the Act, on the ground of the loss to English commerce involved in a struggle with America, and of the difficulties and dangers of a war with that country, which would probably be aided by France and Spain. After speeches from Grenville and Pitt, his motion was carried by a majority of 108. On the third reading of the Bill, there was a violent debate. Pitt again deprecated a war with America. But Grenville still insisted that the expense of the Seven Years' War justified the taxation of America, and that, therefore, the Act should be enforced. "If the tax," he said, "was still to be laid on, I would lay it on." The motion for repeal, however, was carried by a larger majority than on the first reading. By the aid of the independent Peers the Bill was passed in the House of Lords by thirty-four votes. At the same time, the obnoxious duties which had been imposed on the foreign trade of the colonists were altered or removed, and the restrictions upon their trade with some ports in Dominica and Jamaica were abolished. On the whole, America received with expressions of satisfaction and loyalty what had been done by England. Massachusetts remonstrated against the punishment of the rioters, and New York positively refused to obey the clause in the American Mutiny Act, which required the colonists to supply the English troops with some of the necessaries of life. For this act of disobedience the New York Assembly was afterwards temporarily suspended by Act of Parliament.

In 1767 Townshend, as Chancellor of the Exchequer, again attempted to raise a revenue in America by imposing import duties on glass, paper, red and white lead, painters' colours, and tea. He computed that they would yield between £30,000 and £40,000 a year. This Act passed both houses. The receipt of this news provoked fresh opposition in America. In February, 1768, the Assembly of Massachusetts, in spite of the opposition of the Governor, Bernard, sent a circular letter to the Colonies urging resistance to these duties. For this the Assembly was dissolved by the Colonial Secretary, Lord Hillesborough, in the beginning of July. At the same time there was a riot in Boston owing to the attempt of the Custom House authorities to exact the dues on the cargo of a ship called *The Liberty*. A letter was also received from Lord Hillesborough stating that British troops and men-of-war had been ordered to Boston to maintain order. Then, on the refusal of Governor Bernard to convene a new Assembly without orders from home, a Convention of deputies from the districts of Massachusetts met in Boston. On the day of the dissolution of this Convention, the troops landed in Boston. During this time associations to prevent the use of English goods were formed throughout the Colonies, and in many places there were quarrels between the local Assembly and the Governor.

Parliament met in November, 1768. The action of the Assembly of Massachusetts and of the Boston rioters was condemned, and an address was voted to the King, urging that full information should be collected, and that, if necessary, an obsolete statute of Henry VIII. should be revived, which provided for the trial in England of persons accused of treason outside England. The alleged reason for this proposal was that verdicts could not be obtained from an American jury. At the same time, Bernard, who was a most unpopular Governor, was made a Baronet.

In May, 1769, eight days before the close of the session, the Ministry decided that, whatever might be done during the next session about the repeal of the obnoxious duties, that on tea, at least, should not be removed, and this decision was communicated to the Colonies by Lord Hillesborough.

The next session commenced in January, 1770. In the speech from the throne the term "highly unwarrantable" was applied to the proceedings in America. Chatham deprecated this expression, again lauded the spirit of the Americans, and advocated a conciliatory policy towards them.

The news that the Government meditated an enforcement of the statute of Henry VIII. produced fresh
disturbances in America. The use of English imports
was prevented by violence, and all informers, and all
who in any way aided Government, were tarred and
feathered. In March, 1770, Lord North declared his
readiness to abolish all the duties except that on tea.
The decision of the Cabinet to make this concession
had been communicated by Lord Hillesborough in 1769
in a Circular Letter to the Colonial Governors. The
letter stated that the Government entertained no design
to propose to Parliament to lay any further taxes on
America for the purpose of raising a revenue. Lord
North said that, in the face of the violence of the
Americans, he could not go further in the way of
concession. He also urged that the cost of tea was
diminished to the Americans because, when it was imposed at threepence in the pound, a duty of nearly one
shilling a pound, which was formerly levied in England,
had been taken off in the interest of the East India
Company for a period of five years. This was in 1767,
and in 1772 the Act was renewed for another five years.
The Opposition advocated the total repeal of the duties
on the ground that it was foolish to irritate America
by continuing a duty which, partly by smuggling, partly
by the determination of America to import nothing
from England, had during the last year brought in
only £300. Burke spoke in this sense, but the motion
for a partial repeal was carried. On the same day there
was a violent affray between the town-people and the
English troops in Boston. It must be recorded, to the
credit of American justice, that Captain Preston and

his soldiers were acquitted on trial. The concessions made by Lord North were sufficient to restore tranquillity throughout a great part of America for the three years which followed. Commercial activity was restored, except in the matter of tea, which the Americans refused to buy. But it still rankled that the unprofitable tea duty had been retained at the instance of the King, as an assertion of England's right to levy taxes. As before, so now, it was in Massachusetts that the discontent was most pronounced. Government should have taken advantage of this period to restore the old bonds of union with America. But George III. would not renounce his right, and Lord North would not, or could not, resist him.

In 1773 the East India Company applied to England for a loan of one and a half millions sterling. The illicit tea traffic of the Colonies had spoilt their sales of tea, of which they had a large stock lying in their warehouses. Lord North proposed to grant in perpetuity a full drawback of the English duty on all tea of the East India Company exported to America, and also to allow the Company to export direct on their own account. This proposal was carried, and in consequence the Americans could purchase tea at a lower price than they had paid before the colonial duty was imposed. But the irritation caused by the presence of the English revenue officers had not died away in Massachusetts and Virginia. In Rhode Island, a King's ship employed in the repression of smuggling had been destroyed. The Assembly of Massachusetts was irritated at the refusal of England to accede to its request for the removal of Hutchinson and Oliver, the

Governor and Lieutenant-Governor, some of whose private correspondence had been made public, showing that they were in favour of a repressive policy on the part of England. When the ships with the East India Company's tea on board arrived in Boston harbour, they were boarded, and the tea was thrown into the sea. When the news of this outrage reached England Lord North proposed that from June 1st "it should not be lawful for any person to lade or unlade, to ship or unship, any goods from any quay or wharf within Boston harbour." Power was to be reserved to the King of restoring to Boston its privileges as a harbour, so soon as order was restored there, and compensation made to the East India Company for the tea destroyed. Burke opposed this measure, but it was passed. At the same time a Bill was passed making the Council of Massachusetts nominative instead of elective, and transferring to the Governor the power of appointing and removing the judges and other officers of the law who had previously been elected by the Council. A Bill was also passed for quartering and billeting troops throughout the Colonies. This attack on chartered rights alarmed all the Colonies, who determined to unite with Massachusetts for the defence of their liberties. Burke delivered his speech on American Taxation in support of a motion for the repeal of the tea duty which obtained only forty-nine votes. This was in April, 1774.

It was not only the Boston Port Bill and the attack on the Charter of Massachusetts that irritated the Colonies. By the misrepresentations of Governor Hutchinson and his successor, General Gage, public men in

England were led to talk openly of the Americans as cowards. At the instigation of the popular party in Virginia, the first of June, on which day the Boston Port Act was to come into force, was observed as a day of national fasting and prayer. Subscription lists were opened for the relief of the people of Boston. A 'solemn league and covenant' was entered into for the exclusion of English manufactures. In Massachusetts the people refused to give effect to the new constitution. General Gage thought it prudent to fortify himself on a neck of land connecting Boston with the open country. Twelve Colonies agreed to send delegates to *a General Congress* in Philadelphia early in September. Each Colony, no matter how many delegates it sent, was to have one vote. They met to the number of fifty-five, mostly lawyers, in September, a deputy from Virginia being chosen President. They drew up a *Declaration of Rights* claiming that the privileges of Englishmen, which they had never renounced, were still theirs. On that ground they demanded the repeal of recent Acts such as that which changed the government of Massachusetts. Until their request was granted they determined to import nothing from Great Britain after Dec. 1st, 1774, and to export nothing thither after September 10th, 1775. At the same time addresses were forwarded to the people and the Sovereign of Great Britain, and also to the inhabitants of Canada, who were supposed to be discontented with a form of Government recently created for them by Great Britain. The Congress closed its sittings in October with a resolution to reassemble in May, 1775. Meanwhile there had occurred in Massachusetts the striking

phenomenon noted by Burke.[1]   " The time arrived for
appointing the Council according to the new law; but
of the members nominated by the Governor, though
amounting only to thirty-six, there were found only
twenty-four friends of British connection who were
willing to incur the odium of taking the necessary
oaths.   The Council, therefore, could not be constituted.
In these circumstances, the Governor recalled the writs
for the new Assembly which was to meet in October;
but the members already elected voted the proclamation
illegal, and in default of the Governor's appearance to
inaugurate the Assembly with the usual formalities,
they declared themselves a provincial Congress, and
proceeded forthwith to exercise, not only the functions
of a legislative body, but to assume the powers of the
Executive Government.   They formed a Committee of
Safety, which organized a militia force, appointed the
officers, received reports, and directed the sheriffs and
collectors of taxes to retain the proceeds of the public
taxes, subject to their orders.   General Gage issued
a proclamation, denouncing this Assembly and their
acts as seditious and treasonable.   The proclamation
was treated with contempt, and the orders of the
Committee were implicitly obeyed."[2]   The military
preparations of Gage excited the indignation of the
people, and it seemed as if a conflict might occur at
any moment.

After the dissolution of the English Parliament in
September, 1774, the Ministry returned to power with a
large majority.   The people shared the feeling of the King

[1] P. 24.

[2] Massey, *History of England under George III.*, vol. ii., ch. 18

that a policy of concession had been tried and had failed, and that nothing remained but to coerce America. Parliament met in November, but business did not really begin until after the Christmas holidays. On January 20, Chatham urged, in the House of Lords, that resistance to what was now a united America was impossible. He therefore advised Parliament to conciliate America while there was yet time, by yielding the demands of the Philadelphia Congress. This proposal was rejected. He then presented to the Lords a " Provisional Bill for settling the troubles in America," which he had drawn up in consultation with Franklin, after the rejection of his first proposal. He proposed to reaffirm the sovereignty of England in matters of Imperial concern, and, if America recognized this sovereignty, to renounce the right of taxing for revenue. He proposed, further, that a new congress of delegates should meet at Philadelphia, and provide for the due recognition of England's sovereignty, and for a spontaneous grant in perpetuity towards the reduction of the English debt. The extraordinary jurisdiction of Admiralty Courts was to be abolished, charges of murder were to be heard in the province where the offence was committed, and the Coercion Acts, passed since 1764, were to be repealed. The Bill was immediately rejected, but it was printed and circulated for the opinion of the public. In February, Lord North proposed that if a colonial legislature proposed a provision, which the King and Parliament should approve, for the expenses of its own government and of the common defence, Parliament should abstain from taxing the province so long as that provision lasted. This measure was passed. But what-

ever good effect it might have had was prevented by the
association with it of fresh measures for fettering the
trade of the Colonies, in revenge for the non-exportation
and importation agreement. Votes were at the same
time taken for an increase of the English military and
naval forces. Burke moved his resolution on March
22nd. The substance of his speech is as follows :—

Pp. 2-8.   The Commons had sent up to the Lords a bill for restraining
the trade of certain Colonies with Great Britain, Ireland, and
the British Islands in the West Indies, and for restricting their
right to carry on fisheries in Newfoundland. This bill was
returned to the Commons, who thus fortunately obtained an
opportunity of reconsidering their American policy. Burke
entered Parliament at a time when a policy of conciliation
towards America was in favour. He formed a theory of his
own on the subject, from which he has never wavered amid all
the unfortunate changes of Parliamentary opinion and policy.
It is now said that instead of finding fault with whatever the
Government does, he ought to propose a definite scheme of his
own. As a general rule, he thinks it unwise for private individuals to draw up schemes of government. Public misfortunes,
however, justify individuals in doing what in ordinary times it
would be unbecoming for them to undertake. There is nothing
in Burke's position to command acceptance for his proposals, so
they will at least be judged on their own merits. He proposes
to restore peace and confidence by meeting America in a spirit
of conciliation. He does not think that Lord North's scheme
will work ; but at any rate that scheme is a confession that
England ought to grant something to America, and that her
mode of dealing with that country hitherto has been objection-
able. Concessions are always made, most properly, by the
stronger party. Before deciding what is best to be done, it will
be necessary to review the circumstances of America. For the
proper form of government for that country, as for all countries,
must be determined by its circumstances.

Pp. 8-17.   Humanity and interest alike require us to treat with consideration a country possessing such a large and growing population. In little more than half a century the value of England's exports to the Colonies increased twelvefold. In fact, at the time of Burke's speech, England exported to the Colonies alone nearly as much as at the beginning of the century she had exported to the whole world. In 1772, the exports to a single Colony had risen to the value of what was exported in 1704 to all the Colonies. There have been times when England would have been starved if it had not been for the corn which she derived from America. When we consider the spirit with which the Americans have carried on their fisheries, we must rather admire the spirit of a free people than complain of their occasional excesses. Burke deprecates the use of force, because the effect of a victory over America would at most be temporary—because England might not gain the victory—because a struggle would in any case impoverish America, and weaken England—and because experience is in favour of a policy of conciliation.

We must also consider the temper of the Americans. From Pp. 17-23. their first settlement they have been jealous of freedom, and, as descendants of Englishmen, they naturally understand by freedom the right to tax themselves. The spirit of a free people was strengthened in them by the popular form of their government. Their natural feeling of independence is further strengthened by their religion. All Protestants are averse from arbitrary authority, and the North American colonists are Protestants of the most extreme type. It is true that in the Southern Colonies there is an Established English Church ; but there the colonists are slave-owners, and as such are necessarily haughty and independent. The study of law again is very general in America, and it is apt to make people formidable to government. Lastly, it has to be remembered that the control of the English Government can never be so effectual at a distance of 3000 miles as it is at home.

It is evident that the discontent of such a people is not to be Pp. 23-30. treated lightly. It is somewhat alarming to think that America should discover, as she is now discovering, that she can disregard our punitive measures, and can provide for the management of her own affairs, and for the preservation of order in her own borders. It is equally important to remember that an English attack upon the freedom of America must weaken the hold of the English upon their own liberties.

It is impossible to change the spirit of the Americans by removing its causes. We cannot limit their numbers. We may exclude the growing population from the districts subject to our authority, but that will only turn them into wandering savages who would be a danger to our dominions. We can of course impoverish them by fettering their trade. But in impoverishing them we should impoverish ourselves too, and the poverty to which we reduce them will but goad them to rebellion. Men of English origin will never consent to be slaves. We cannot change their religion or their education. We cannot substitute a military despotism for their popular assemblies, nor would it be profitable or safe to do so if we could. If it is proposed to bring down the pride of the Virginians by enfranchising their slaves, the answer is that the slaves might not wish for freedom, and that the Virginians may anticipate us by freeing them themselves, and arming them against us. Finally, America cannot be brought nearer to us so as to be brought more directly under our control.

Pp. 30-33. But it may be said that, if we cannot change the Americans, we can punish them. Burke says criminal procedure is not applicable on such a large scale. You cannot charge or bring to trial millions of people. It is moreover an insult to a nation to treat it as a criminal. A member of an Empire does not impugn the imperial authority by claiming a privilege. Rather, in the act of claiming it, he recognizes the power of the imperial authority. If the subordinate communities of our Empire are to have no privileges, they are slaves, and will soon refuse to belong to such an Empire. In all quarrels between herself and her dependents, England is the judge, and is likely to be too partial to herself. She must remember that there are times when equity requires her not even to exercise her undoubted rights. In this case the right is not undoubted. England first decides that she has the right to tax, and then punishes America for denying the right. That we cannot take criminal proceedings against America is proved by the fact that after charging Massachusetts

with the crime of rebellion, instead of proceeding against the
rebels at law, we have dealt with the Colony as if it were a
hostile power.

If we can neither change the Americans nor punish them, we Pp. 33-39.
must conciliate them by ceasing to tax them in a Parliament
where they are not represented. Whether we have the right to
tax them or not does not matter in the least. It is often in-
equitable, unwise, or imprudent to assert even an undoubted
right. Even if the ancestors of the colonists had contracted for
themselves and their descendants to be slaves, it would still be
advisable to grant freedom to those descendants when they demanded it, rather than to disturb the peace of the Empire. To
satisfy the Colonies and to protect ourselves against a temptation
to unconstitutional action in the future, we should declare once
for all that they are to have the benefit of English constitutional
principles. The opposition to Burke's scheme is prompted by an
unreasonable fear that, if the taxes are repealed, the Americans
will immediately cry out against the control of their trade
by England. Burke says that it is very unfair to punish the
Americans merely because you think that they are going to do
something. They quarrelled not with commercial restrictions
but with taxes. You cannot say what they will do when the
taxes are removed until you have removed them. Experience
would lead us to suppose that by removing grievances we make
not enemies but friends.

The policy which Burke recommends is in accordance with Pp. 39-46.
constitutional precedents, and, if England wishes to maintain
her Empire, she cannot do better than act on the principles by
which she acquired it. England has succeeded in making
Ireland loyal exactly in proportion as she has shared her own
privileges with her. Ireland has contributed generously because
she has been allowed to contribute freely. The same was the
case with Wales. It was a burden to England so long as we
treated it as we are now treating America. It became a peace-
able country as soon as we recognized the rights of its inhabitants. The same policy was at the same time adopted and with
the same results towards the County Palatine of Chester, and
later with regard to Durham. In all cases England has recog-

nized the right of the subordinate provinces of the Empire to tax themselves. Burke wishes to recognize the same right in the Americans. They cannot be represented in the English Parliaments, but experience has shown that they both can and will tax themselves for the benefit of the Empire, and that, except by free grants, they cannot be made to contribute to the support of the Empire at all.

Pp. 46-57. Burke wishes Parliament to record that the Americans though unrepresented in the English Parliament have been grieved by taxes imposed upon them by that Parliament, and have in consequence disturbed the peace of the Empire—that no means have been devised for securing representation to the Americans in England, but that the American Assemblies are competent to make grants and have often shown themselves willing to make them, and that attempts to get money from them in any other way have failed. The truth of these propositions is proved by facts, and by the records of Parliament itself. These things being so, Burke proposes to repeal the Acts by which duties are levied in America instead of in England—to repeal the Act depriving Boston of the privileges of a harbour—to annul the punitive measures passed against Massachusetts—and to restrict the operation of the statute of Henry VIII. Burke further proposes to make properly appointed judges in America irremovable except by the Sovereign in Council upon a formal request from America. Lastly, he proposes to amend the constitution and procedure of the Admiralty Courts charged with the enforcement of the Law of Navigation.

Pp. 57-end. If it be objected that England can no more legislate for unrepresented Colonies than she can tax them, Burke replies (1) It is not he but Parliament that has asserted taxation without representation to be a grievance. (2) This principle has been recognized as compatible with an absolute *or* a limited sovereignty on the part of England. (3) In the case of Durham the grievance related solely to taxation without representation. (4) In the case of Durham and Chester Parliament did not trouble to define its sovereignty, but recognized that it could not tax those who were not represented. We are not to judge of what the Americans will do by expressions they may have used in the heat of passion, and, even if the abandonment of the right to tax involves the abandonment of the right to legislate, yet it does not follow that America will rebel against our laws. Men act much more out of regard to their own interests than to mere logical consistency. The Americans will make some sacrifices in order to belong to the Empire, because they gain in importance by belonging to it. Englishmen must not think their Empire dissolved because a relative independence is granted to different parts of it.

Burke deprecates Lord North's plan because such a plan has never been tried—because it will put power into the hands of the Ministers—because it is impracticable—and because an attempt to enforce it would lead to dissension and war. Burke proposes to do what experience shows it to be safe to do, viz., to trust to the voluntary liberality of America. People to whom membership of the Empire is valuable will make sacrifices to retain that membership. If England does her duty, her dependents will not fail to do theirs. Moral forces are more powerful than political regulations.

Burke's proposals were rejected by the Commons as were those of Chatham by the Lords. " With the rejection of these efforts at conciliation began the great struggle which ended eight years later in the severance of the American Colonies from the British Crown." [1]

[1] Green.

BURKE'S SPEECH ON
CONCILIATION WITH AMERICA

SPEECH ON MOVING HIS RESOLUTIONS

FOR

CONCILIATION WITH THE COLONIES.

MARCH 22, 1775.

I HOPE, Sir, that, notwithstanding the austerity of the
Chair, ycur good-nature will incline you to some degree of
indulgence towards human frailty. You will not think it
unnatural, that those who have an object depending, which
strongly engages their hopes and fears, should be somewhat
inclined to superstition. As I came into the House full of
anxiety about the event of my motion, I found, to my infinite surprise, that the grand penal bill, by which we had
passed sentence on the trade and sustenance of America,
10 is to be returned to us from the other House. I do confess,
I could not help looking on this event as a fortunate omen.
I look upon it as a sort of providential favour ; by which
we are put once more in possession of our deliberative
capacity, upon a business so very questionable in its nature,
so very uncertain in its issue. By the return of this bill,
which seemed to have taken its flight for ever, we are at
this very instant nearly as free to choose a plan for our
American government as we were on the first day of the
session. If, Sir, we incline to the side of conciliation, we
20 are not at all embarrassed (unless we please to make ourselves so) by any incongruous mixture of coercion and
restraint. We are therefore called upon, as it were by a

2

superior warning voice, again to attend to America; to attend to the whole of it together; and to review the subject with an unusual degree of care and calmness.

Surely it is an awful subject; or there is none so on this side of the grave. When I first had the honour of a seat in this House, the affairs of that continent pressed themselves upon us, as the most important and most delicate object of parliamentary attention. My little share in this great deliberation oppressed me. I found myself a partaker in a very high trust; and having no sort of reason to rely 10 on the strength of my natural abilities for the proper execution of that trust, I was obliged to take more than common pains to instruct myself in everything which relates to our colonies. I was not less under the necessity of forming some fixed ideas concerning the general policy of the British Empire. Something of this sort seemed to be indispensable; in order, amidst so vast a fluctuation of passions and opinions, to concentre my thoughts; to ballast my conduct; to preserve me from being blown about by every wind of fashionable doctrine. I really did not 20 think it safe, or manly, to have fresh principles to seek upon every fresh mail which should arrive from America.

At that period I had the fortune to find myself in perfect concurrence with a large majority in this House. Bowing under that high authority, and penetrated with the sharpness and strength of that early impression, I have continued ever since, without the least deviation, in my original sentiments. Whether this be owing to an obstinate perseverance in error, or to a religious adherence to what appears to me truth and reason, it is in your equity to judge.   30

Sir, Parliament having an enlarged view of objects, made, during this interval, more frequent changes in their sentiments and their conduct, than could be justified in a particular person upon the contracted scale of private information. But though I do not hazard anything approaching to censure on the motives of former parliaments

to all those alterations, one fact is undoubted,—that under
them the state of America has been kept in continual
agitation. Everything administered as remedy to the
public complaint, if it did not produce, was at least
followed by, an heightening of the distemper; until, by a
variety of experiments, that important country has been
brought into her present situation;—a situation which I
will not miscall, which I dare not name; which I scarcely
know how to comprehend in the terms of any description.

10 In this posture, Sir, things stood at the beginning of the
session. About that time, a worthy member of great parliamentary experience, who, in the year 1766, filled the chair of
the American committee with much ability, took me aside;
and, lamenting the present aspect of our politics, told me,
things were come to such a pass, that our former methods of
proceeding in the House would be no longer tolerated. That
the public tribunal (never too indulgent to a long and
unsuccessful opposition) would now scrutinize our conduct
with unusual severity. That the very vicissitudes and

20 shiftings of ministerial measures, instead of convicting their
authors of inconstancy and want of system, would be taken
as an occasion of charging us with a predetermined discontent, which nothing could satisfy; whilst we accused every
measure of vigour as cruel, and every proposal of lenity as
weak and irresolute. The public, he said, would not have
patience to see us play the game out with our adversaries :
we must produce our hand. It would be expected, that
those who for many years had been active in such affairs
should show, that they had formed some clear and decided

30 idea of the principles of colony government; and were
capable of drawing out something like a platform of the
ground which might be laid for future and permanent
tranquillity.

I felt the truth of what my hon. friend represented; but
I felt my situation too. His application might have been
made with far greater propriety to many other gentlemen.

No man was indeed ever better disposed, or worse qualified, for such an undertaking, than myself. Though I gave so far in to his opinion, that I immediately threw my thoughts into a sort of parliamentary form, I was by no means equally ready to produce them. It generally argues some degree of natural impotence of mind, or some want of knowledge of the world, to hazard plans of government except from a seat of authority. Propositions are made, not only ineffectually, but somewhat disreputably, when the minds of men are not properly disposed for their 10 reception; and for my part, I am not ambitious of ridicule; not absolutely a candidate for disgrace.

Besides, Sir, to speak the plain truth, I have in general no very exalted opinion of the virtue of paper government; nor of any politics in which the plan is to be wholly separated from the execution. But when I saw that anger and violence prevailed every day more and more; and that things were hastening towards an incurable alienation of our colonies; I confess my caution gave way. I felt this, as one of those few moments in which decorum yields to a 20 higher duty. Public calamity is a mighty leveller; and there are occasions when any, even the slightest, chance of doing good, must be laid hold on, even by the most inconsiderable person.

To restore order and repose to an empire so great and so distracted as ours, is, merely in the attempt, an undertaking that would ennoble the flights of the highest genius, and obtain pardon for the efforts of the meanest understanding. Struggling a good while with these thoughts, by degrees I felt myself more firm. I derived, at length, some confi- 30 dence from what in other circumstances usually produces timidity. I grew less anxious, even from the idea of my own insignificance. For, judging of what you are by what you ought to be, I persuaded myself that you would not reject a reasonable proposition because it had nothing but its reason to recommend it. On the other hand, being

totally destitute of all shadow of influence, natural or adventitious, I was very sure, that, if my proposition were
futile or dangerous; if it were weakly conceived, or im-
properly timed, there was nothing exterior to it, of power
to awe, dazzle, or delude you. You will see it just as it is:
and you will treat it just as it deserves.

The proposition is peace. Not peace through the medium
of war; not peace to be hunted through the labyrinth of
intricate and endless negotiations; not peace to arise out of
10 universal discord, fomented from principle, in all parts of
the empire; not peace to depend on the juridical determination of perplexing questions, or the precise marking the
shadowy boundaries of a complex government. It is simple
peace; sought in its natural course, and in its ordinary
haunts.—It is peace sought in the spirit of peace; and laid
in principles purely pacific. I propose, by removing the
ground of the difference, and by restoring the *former unsuspecting confidence of the colonies in the mother country*, to
give permanent satisfaction to your people; and (far from a
20 scheme of ruling by discord) to reconcile them to each other
in the same act, and by the bond of the very same interest
which reconciles them to British government.

My idea is nothing more. Refined policy ever has been
the parent of confusion; and ever will be so, as long as the
world endures. Plain good intention, which is as easily
discovered at the first view, as fraud is surely detected at
last, is, let me say, of no mean force in the government of
mankind. Genuine simplicity of heart is an healing and
cementing principle. My plan, therefore, being formed
30 upon the most simple grounds imaginable, may disappoint
some people, when they hear it. It has nothing to recommend it to the pruriency of curious ears. There is nothing
at all new and captivating in it. It has nothing of the
splendour of the project, which has been lately laid upon
your table by the noble lord in the blue riband. It does
not propose to fill your lobby with squabbling colony agents,

who will require the interposition of your mace, at every instant, to keep the peace amongst them. It does not institute a magnificent auction of finance, where captivated provinces come to general ransom by bidding against each other, until you knock down the hammer, and determine a proportion of payments beyond all the powers of algebra to equalize and settle.

The plan which I shall presume to suggest, derives, however, one great advantage from the proposition and registry of that noble lord's project. The idea of conciliation is 10 admissible. First, the House, in accepting the resolution moved by the noble lord, has admitted, notwithstanding the menacing front of our address, notwithstanding our heavy bills of pains and penalties—that we do not think ourselves precluded from all ideas of free grace and bounty.

The House has gone further; it has declared conciliation admissible, *previous* to any submission on the part of America. It has even shot a good deal beyond that mark, and has admitted, that the complaints of our former mode of exerting the right of taxation were not wholly unfounded. 20 That right thus exerted is allowed to have had something reprehensible in it; something unwise, or something grievous; since, in the midst of our heat and resentment, we, of ourselves, have proposed a capital alteration; and, in order to get rid of what seemed so very exceptionable, have instituted a mode that is altogether new; one that is, indeed, wholly alien from all the ancient methods and forms of parliament.

The *principle* of this proceeding is large enough for my purpose. The means proposed by the noble lord for carry- 30 ing his ideas into execution, I think, indeed, are very indifferently suited to the end; and this I shall endeavour to show you before I sit down. But, for the present, I take my ground on the admitted principle. I mean to give peace. Peace implies reconciliation; and, where there has been a material dispute, reconciliation does in a manner always

imply concession on the one part or on the other. In this
state of things I make no difficulty in affirming that the
proposal ought to originate from us. Great and acknowledged force is not impaired, either in effect or in opinion,
by an unwillingness to exert itself. The superior power
may offer peace with honour and with safety. Such an
offer from such a power will be attributed to magnanimity.
But the concessions of the weak are the concessions of fear.
When such a one is disarmed, he is wholly at the mercy
10 of his superior; and he loses for ever that time and those
chances, which, as they happen to all men, are the strength
and resources of all inferior power.

The capital leading questions on which you must this day
decide, are these two: First, whether you ought to concede;
and secondly, what your concession ought to be. On the
first of these questions we have gained (as I have just taken
the liberty of observing to you) some ground. But I am
sensible that a good deal more is still to be done. Indeed,
Sir, to enable us to determine both on the one and the other
20 of these great questions with a firm and precise judgment,
I think it may be necessary to consider distinctly the true
nature and the peculiar circumstances of the object which
we have before us. Because after all our struggle, whether
we will or not, we must govern America according to that
nature, and to those circumstances; and not according to
our own imaginations; nor according to abstract ideas of
right; by no means according to mere general theories of
government, the resort to which appears to me, in our
present situation, no better than arrant trifling. I shall
30 therefore endeavour, with your leave, to lay before you
some of the most material of these circumstances in as full
and as clear a manner as I am able to state them.

The first thing that we have to consider with regard to
the nature of the object is—the number of people in the
colonies. I have taken for some years a good deal of pains
on that point. I can by no calculation justify myself in

placing the number below two millions of inhabitants of our own European blood and colour; besides at least 500,000 others, who form no inconsiderable part of the strength and opulence of the whole. This, Sir, is, I believe, about the true number. There is no occasion to exaggerate, where plain truth is of so much weight and importance. But whether I put the present numbers too high or too low, is a matter of little moment. Such is the strength with which population shoots in that part of the world, that state the numbers as high as we will, whilst the dispute continues, 10 the exaggeration ends. Whilst we are discussing any given magnitude, they are grown to it. Whilst we spend our time in deliberating on the mode of governing two millions, we shall find we have millions more to manage. Your children do not grow faster from infancy to manhood, than they spread from families to communities, and from villages to nations.

I put this consideration of the present and the growing numbers in the front of our deliberation; because, Sir, this consideration will make it evident to a blunter discernment 20 than yours, that no partial, narrow, contracted, pinched, occasional system will be at all suitable to such an object. It will show you, that it is not to be considered as one of those *minima* [*trifles*] which are out of the eye and consideration of the law; not a paltry excrescence of the state; not a mean dependent, who may be neglected with little damage, and provoked with little danger. It will prove that some degree of care and caution is required in the handling such an object; it will show that you ought not, in reason, to trifle with so large a mass of the interests and feelings of the 30 human race. You could at no time do so without guilt; and be assured you will not be able to do it long with impunity.

But the population of this country, the great and growing population, though a very important consideration, will lose much of its weight, if not combined with other circumstances. The commerce of your colonies is out of all pro-

portion beyond the numbers of the people. This ground of their commerce indeed has been trod some days ago, and with great ability, by a distinguished person, at your bar. This gentleman, after thirty-five years—it is so long since he first appeared at the same place to plead for the commerce of Great Britain—has come again before you to plead the same cause, without any other effect of time, than, that to the fire of imagination and extent of erudition, which even then marked him as one of the first literary characters of his age,
10 he has added a consummate knowledge in the commercial interest of his country, formed by a long course of enlightened and discriminating experience.

Sir, I should be inexcusable in coming after such a person with any detail, if a great part of the members who now fill the House had not the misfortune to be absent when he appeared at your bar. Besides, Sir, I propose to take the matter at periods of time somewhat different from his. There is, if I mistake not, a point of view, from whence if you will look at this subject, it is impossible that it should
20 not make an impression upon you.

I have in my hand two accounts ; one a comparative state of the export trade of England to its colonies, as it stood in the year 1704, and as it stood in the year 1772. The other a state of the export trade of this country to its colonies alone, as it stood in 1772, compared with the whole trade of England to all parts of the world (the colonies included) in the year 1704. They are from good vouchers ; the latter period from the accounts on your table, the earlier from an original manuscript of Davenant, who first established the inspector-
30 general's office, which has been ever since his time so abundant a source of parliamentary information.

The export trade to the colonies consists of three great branches. The African, which, terminating almost wholly in the colonies, must be put to the account of their commerce ; the West Indian ; and the North American. All these are so interwoven, that the attempt to separate them, would tear to pieces the contexture of the whole ; and if not entirely destroy, would very much depreciate the value of all the parts. I therefore consider these three denominations to be, what in effect they are, one trade.

The trade to the colonies, taken on the export side, at the beginning of this century, that is, in the year 1704, stood thus :

Exports to North America, and the West Indies - - - - - -	£483,265	
To Africa - - - - - -	86,665	10
	£569,930	

In the year 1772, which I take as a middle year between the highest and lowest of those lately laid on your table, the account was as follows :

To North America, and the West Indies	£4,791,734	
To Africa - - - - - -	866,398	
To which if you add the export trade from Scotland, which had in 1704 no existence - - - - -	364,000	
	£6,022,132	20

From five hundred and odd thousand, it has grown to six millions. It has increased no less than twelve-fold. This is the state of the colony trade, as compared with itself at these two periods, within this century ;—and this is matter for meditation. But this is not all. Examine my second account. See how the export trade to the colonies alone in 1772 stood in the other point of view, that is, as compared to the whole trade of England in 1704.

The whole export trade of England, including that to the colonies, in 1704	£6,509,000	30
Export to the colonies alone, in 1772 -	6,024,000	
Difference	£485,000	

The trade with America alone is now within less than £500,000 of being equal to what this great commercial nation, England, carried on at the beginning of this century with the whole world ! If I had taken the largest year of those on your table, it would rather have exceeded. But, it will be said, is not this American trade an unnatural protuberance, that has drawn the juices from the rest of the body ? The reverse. It is the very food that has nourished every other part into its present magnitude. Our general 10 trade has been greatly augmented, and augmented more or less in almost every part to which it ever extended ; but with this material difference, that of the six millions which in the beginning of the century constituted the whole mass of our export commerce, the colony trade was but one twelfth part ; it is now (as a part of sixteen millions) considerably more than a third of the whole. This is the relative proportion of the importance of the colonies at these two periods : and all reasoning concerning our mode of treating them must have this proportion as its basis, or it is a 20 reasoning weak, rotten, and sophistical.

Mr. Speaker, I cannot prevail on myself to hurry over this great consideration. It is good for us to be here. We stand where we have an immense view of what is, and what is past. Clouds, indeed, and darkness rest upon the future. Let us, however, before we descend from this noble eminence, reflect that this growth of our national prosperity has happened within the short period of the life of man. It has happened within sixty-eight years. There are those alive whose memory might touch the two extremities. For 30 instance, my Lord Bathurst might remember all the stages of the progress. He was in 1704 of an age at least to be made to comprehend such things. He was then old enough *acta parentum jam legere, et quæ sit potuit cognoscere virtus* [*to study the doings of his forefathers, and to learn the meaning of virtue*]—Suppose, Sir, that the angel of this auspicious youth, foreseeing the many virtues, which made him one of the most amiable, as he is one of the most fortunate, men of his age, had opened to him in vision, that when, in the fourth generation, the third prince of the House of Brunswick had sat twelve years on the throne of that nation, which (by the happy issue of moderate and healing counsels) was to be made Great Britain, he should see his son, Lord Chancellor of England, turn back the current of hereditary dignity to its fountain, and raise him to a higher rank of peerage, whilst he enriched the family with a new one—If amidst these bright and happy scenes of domestic honour and 10 prosperity, that angel should have drawn up the curtain, and unfolded the rising glories of his country, and whilst he was gazing with admiration on the then commercial grandeur of England, the genius should point out to him a little speck, scarce visible in the mass of the national interest, a small seminal principle, rather than a formed body, and should tell him—"Young man, there is America—which at this day serves for little more than to amuse you with stories of savage men, and uncouth manners; yet shall, before you taste of death, show itself equal to the whole of that com- 20 merce which now attracts the envy of the world. Whatever England has been growing to by a progressive increase of improvement, brought in by varieties of people, by succession of civilizing conquests and civilizing settlements in a series of seventeen hundred years, you shall see as much added to her by America in the course of a single life!" If this state of his country had been foretold to him, would it not require all the sanguine credulity of youth, and all the fervid glow of enthusiasm, to make him believe it? Fortunate man, he has lived to see it! Fortunate indeed, if he lives to see 30 nothing that shall vary the prospect, and cloud the setting of his day!

Excuse me, Sir, if turning from such thoughts I resume this comparative view once more. You have seen it on a large scale; look at it on a small one. I will point out to your attention a particular instance of it in the single province of Pennsylvania. In the year 1704, that province called for £11,459 in value of your commodities, native and foreign. This was the whole. What did it demand in 1772? Why nearly fifty times as much ; for in that year the export to Pennsylvania was £507,909, nearly equal to the export to all the colonies together in the first period.

I choose, Sir, to enter into these minute and particular details ; because generalities, which in all other cases are apt to heighten and raise the subject, have here a tendency to
10 sink it. When we speak of the commerce with our colonies, fiction lags after truth ; invention is unfruitful, and imagination cold and barren.

So far, Sir, as to the importance of the object in view of its commerce, as concerned in the exports from England. If I were to detail the imports, I could show how many enjoyments they procure, which deceive the burthen of life ; how many materials which invigorate the springs of national industry, and extend and animate every part of our foreign and domestic commerce. This would be a curious
20 subject indeed—but I must prescribe bounds to myself in a matter so vast and various.

I pass therefore to the colonies in another point of view, their agriculture. This they have prosecuted with such a spirit, that, besides feeding plentifully their own growing multitude, their annual export of grain, comprehending rice, has some years ago exceeded a million in value. Of their last harvest, I am persuaded they will export much more. At the beginning of the century some of these colonies imported corn from the mother country. For some time past, the Old
30 World has been fed from the New. The scarcity which you have felt would have been a desolating famine, if this child of your old age, with a true filial piety, with a Roman charity, had not put the full breast of its youthful exuberance to the mouth of its exhausted parent.

As to the wealth which the colonies have drawn from the sea by their fisheries, you had all that matter fully opened at your bar. You surely thought these acquisitions of value, for they seemed even to excite your envy; and yet the spirit by which that enterprising employment has been exercised, ought rather, in my opinion, to have raised your esteem and admiration. And pray, Sir, what in the world is equal to it? Pass by the other parts, and look at the manner in which the people of New England have of late carried on the whale fishery. Whilst we follow them among the tumbling mountains of ice, and behold them penetrating into the deepest frozen recesses of Hudson's Bay and Davis's Straits, whilst 10 we are looking for them beneath the arctic circle, we hear that they have pierced into the opposite region of polar cold, that they are at the antipodes, and engaged under the frozen serpent of the south. Falkland Island, which seemed too remote and romantic an object for the grasp of national ambition, is but a stage and resting-place in the progress of their victorious industry. Nor is the equinoctial heat more discouraging to them, than the accumulated winter of both the poles. We know that whilst some of them draw the line and strike the harpoon on the coast of Africa, others run the 20 longitude, and pursue their gigantic game along the coast of Brazil. No sea but what is vexed by their fisheries. No climate that is not witness to their toils. Neither the perseverance of Holland, nor the activity of France, nor the dexterous and firm sagacity of English enterprise, ever carried this most perilous mode of hardy industry to the extent to which it has been pushed by this recent people; a people who are still, as it were, but in the gristle, and not yet hardened into the bone of manhood. When I contemplate these things; when I know that the colonies in general 30 owe little or nothing to any care of ours, and that they are not squeezed into this happy form by the constraints of watchful and suspicious government, but that, through a wise and salutary neglect, a generous nature has been suffered to take her own way to perfection; when I reflect upon these effects, when I see how profitable they have been to us, I feel all the pride of power sink, and all presumption in the wisdom of human contrivances melt and die away within me. My rigour relents. I pardon something to the spirit of liberty.

I am sensible, Sir, that all which I have asserted in my detail, is admitted in the gross; but that quite a different conclusion is drawn from it. America, gentlemen say, is a noble object. It is an object well worth fighting for. Certainly it is, if fighting a people be the best way of gaining
10 them. Gentlemen in this respect will be led to their choice of means by their complexions and their habits. Those who understand the military art, will of course have some predilection for it. Those who wield the thunder of the state, may have more confidence in the efficacy of arms. But I confess, possibly for want of this knowledge, my opinion is much more in favour of prudent management, than of force; considering force not as an odious, but a feeble instrument, for preserving a people so numerous, so active, so growing, so spirited as this, in a profitable and subordinate connexion
20 with us.

First, Sir, permit me to observe, that the use of force alone is but *temporary*. It may subdue for a moment; but it does not remove the necessity of subduing again; and a nation is not governed, which is perpetually to be conquered.

My next objection is its *uncertainty*. Terror is not always the effect of force; and an armament is not a victory. If you do not succeed, you are without resource; for, conciliation failing, force remains; but, force failing, no further hope of reconciliation is left. Power and authority are
30 sometimes bought by kindness; but they can never be begged as alms by an impoverished and defeated violence.

A further objection to force is, that you *impair the object* by your very endeavours to preserve it. The thing you fought for is not the thing which you recover; but depreciated, sunk, wasted, and consumed in the contest. Nothing less will content me, than *whole America*. I do not choose to consume its strength along with our own ; because in all parts it is the British strength that I consume. I do not choose to be caught by a foreign enemy at the end of this exhausting conflict ; and still less in the midst of it. I may escape ; but I can make no insurance against such an event. Let me add, that I do not choose wholly to break the American spirit; because it is the spirit that has made the country.

Lastly, we have no sort of *experience* in favour of force as an instrument in the rule of our colonies. Their growth and 10 their utility has been owing to methods altogether different. Our ancient indulgence has been said to be pursued to a fault. It may be so. But we know if feeling is evidence, that our fault was more tolerable than our attempt to mend it ; and our sin far more salutary than our penitence.

These, Sir, are my reasons for not entertaining that high opinion of untried force, by which many gentlemen, for whose sentiments in other particulars I have great respect, seem to be so greatly captivated. But there is still behind a third consideration concerning this object, which serves to 20 determine my opinion on the sort of policy which ought to be pursued in the management of America, even more than its population and its commerce, I mean its *temper and character.*

In this character of the Americans, a love of freedom is the predominating feature which marks and distinguishes the whole : and as an ardent is always a jealous affection, your colonies become suspicious, restive, and untractable, whenever they see the least attempt to wrest from them by force, or shuffle from them by chicane, what they think the 30 only advantage worth living for. This fierce spirit of liberty is stronger in the English colonies probably than in any other people of the earth ; and this from a great variety of powerful causes ; which, to understand the true temper of their minds, and the direction which this spirit takes, it will not be amiss to lay open somewhat more largely.

First, the people of the colonies are descendants of Englishmen. England, Sir, is a nation, which still I hope respects,
and formerly adored, her freedom. The colonists emigrated
from you when this part of your character was most
predominant; and they took this bias and direction the
moment they parted from your hands. They are therefore
not only devoted to liberty, but to liberty according to
English ideas, and on English principles. Abstract liberty,
like other mere abstractions, is not to be found. Liberty
10 inheres in some sensible object; and every nation has formed
to itself some favourite point, which by way of eminence
becomes the criterion of their happiness. It happened, you
know, Sir, that the great contests for freedom in this
country were from the earliest times chiefly upon the question of taxing. Most of the contests in the ancient
commonwealths turned primarily on the right of election of
magistrates ; or on the balance among the several orders of
the state. The question of money was not with them so
immediate. But in England it was otherwise. On this
20 point of taxes the ablest pens, and most eloquent tongues,
have been exercised ; the greatest spirits have acted and
suffered. In order to give the fullest satisfaction concerning
the importance of this point, it was not only necessary for
those who in argument defended the excellence of the English constitution, to insist on this privilege of granting
money as a dry point of fact, and to prove, that the right
had been acknowledged in ancient parchments, and blind
usages, to reside in a certain body called a House of
Commons. They went much farther ; they attempted to
30 prove, and they succeeded, that in theory it ought to be so,
from the particular nature of a House of Commons, as an
immediate representative of the people ; whether the old
records had delivered this oracle or not. They took infinite
pains to inculcate, as a fundamental principle, that in all
monarchies the people must in effect themselves, mediately
or immediately, possess the power of granting their own

money, or no shadow of liberty could subsist. The colonies
draw from you, as with their life-blood, these ideas and principles. Their love of liberty, as with you, fixed and attached
on this specific point of taxing. Liberty might be safe, or
might be endangered, in twenty other particulars, without
their being much pleased or alarmed. Here they felt its
pulse; and as they found that beat, they thought themselves
sick or sound. I do not say whether they were right or
wrong in applying your general arguments to their own
case. It is not easy indeed to make a monopoly of theorems 10
and corollaries. The fact is, that they did thus apply those
general arguments; and your mode of governing them,
whether through lenity or indolence, through wisdom or
mistake, confirmed them in the imagination, that they, as
well as you, had an interest in these common principles.

They were further confirmed in this pleasing error by the
form of their provincial legislative assemblies. Their governments are popular in a high degree; some are merely
popular; in all, the popular representative is the most
weighty; and this share of the people in their ordinary 20
government never fails to inspire them with lofty sentiments,
and with a strong aversion from whatever tends to deprive
them of their chief importance.

If anything were wanting to this necessary operation of
the form of government, religion would have given it a
complete effect. Religion, always a principle of energy, in
this new people is no way worn out or impaired ; and their
mode of professing it is also one main cause of this free
spirit. The people are Protestants ; and of that kind which
is the most adverse to all implicit submission of mind and 30
opinion. This is a persuasion not only favourable to liberty,
but built upon it. I do not think, Sir, that the reason of
this averseness in the dissenting churches, from all that looks
like absolute government, is so much to be sought in their
religious tenets, as in their history. Every one knows that
the Roman Catholic religion is at least coeval with most of

the governments where it prevails ; that it has generally gone hand in hand with them, and received great favour and every kind of support from authority. The Church of England too was formed from her cradle under the nursing care of regular government. But the dissenting interests have sprung up in direct opposition to all the ordinary powers of the world ; and could justify that opposition only on a strong claim to natural liberty. Their very existence depended on the powerful and unremitted assertion of that
10 claim. All Protestantism, even the most cold and passive, is a sort of dissent. But the religion most prevalent in our northern colonies is a refinement on the principle of resist- ance ; it is the dissidence of dissent, and the Protestantism of the Protestant religion. This religion, under a variety of denominations agreeing in nothing but in the communion of the spirit of liberty, is predominant in most of the northern provinces ; where the Church of England, notwithstanding its legal rights, is in reality no more than a sort of private sect, not composing most probably the tenth of the people.
20 The colonists left England when this spirit was high, and in the emigrants was the highest of all ; and even that stream of foreigners, which has been constantly flowing into these colonies, has, for the greatest part, been composed of dis- senters from the establishments of their several countries, and have brought with them a temper and character far from alien to that of the people with whom they mixed.

Sir, I can perceive by their manner, that some gentlemen object to the latitude of this description ; because in the southern colonies the Church of England forms a large body,
30 and has a regular establishment. It is certainly true. There is, however, a circumstance attending these colonies, which, in my opinion, fully counterbalances this difference, and makes the spirit of liberty still more high and haughty than in those to the northward. It is, that in Virginia and the Carolinas they have a vast multitude of slaves. Where this is the case in any part of the world, those who are free, are

by far the most proud and jealous of their freedom. Freedom is to them not only an enjoyment, but a kind of rank
and privilege. Not seeing there, that freedom, as in countries
where it is a common blessing, and as broad and general
as the air, may be united with much abject toil, with great
misery, with all the exterior of servitude, liberty looks,
amongst them, like something that is more noble and liberal.
I do not mean, Sir, to commend the superior morality of this
sentiment, which has at least as much pride as virtue in it ;
but I cannot alter the nature of man. The fact is so ; and 10
these people of the southern colonies are much more strongly,
and with a higher and more stubborn spirit, attached to
liberty, than those to the northward. Such were all the
ancient commonwealths ; such were our Gothic ancestors ;
such in our days were the Poles; and such will be all
masters of slaves, who are not slaves themselves. In such a
people, the haughtiness of domination combines with the
spirit of freedom, fortifies it, and renders it invincible.

Permit me, Sir, to add another circumstance in our colonies,
which contributes no mean part towards the growth and 20
effect of this untractable spirit. I mean their education. In
no country perhaps in the world is the law so general a
study. The profession itself is numerous and powerful ; and
in most provinces it takes the lead. The greater number of
the deputies sent to the congress were lawyers. But all
who read, and most do read, endeavour to obtain some
smattering in that science. I have been told by an eminent
bookseller, that in no branch of his business, after tracts of
popular devotion, were so many books as those on the law
exported to the plantations. The colonists have now fallen 30
into the way of printing them for their own use. I hear
that they have sold nearly as many of Blackstone's Commentaries in America as in England. General Gage marks
out this disposition very particularly in a letter on your
table. He states, that all the people in his government are
lawyers, or smatterers in law ; and that in Boston they have

been enabled, by successful chicane, wholly to evade many parts of one of your capital penal constitutions. The smartness of debate will say, that this knowledge ought to teach them more clearly the rights of legislature, their obligations to obedience, and the penalties of rebellion. All this is mighty well. But my honourable and learned friend on the floor, who condescends to mark what I say for animadversion, will disdain that ground. He has heard, as well as I, that when great honours and great emoluments do not win over
10 this knowledge to the service of the state, it is a formidable adversary to government. If the spirit be not tamed and broken by these happy methods, it is stubborn and litigious. *Abeunt studia in mores.* [*Pursuits influence character.*] This study renders men acute, inquisitive, dexterous, prompt in attack, ready in defence, full of resources. In other countries, the people, more simple, and of a less mercurial cast, judge of an ill principle in government only by an actual grievance ; here they anticipate the evil, and judge of the pressure of the grievance by the badness of the principle. They augur
20 misgovernment at a distance ; and snuff the approach of tyranny in every tainted breeze.

The last cause of this disobedient spirit in the colonies is hardly less powerful than the rest, as it is not merely moral, but laid deep in the natural constitution of things. Three thousand miles of ocean lie between you and them. No contrivance can prevent the effect of this distance in weakening government. Seas roll, and months pass, between the order and the execution ; and the want of a speedy explanation of a single point is enough to defeat a whole system. You
30 have, indeed, winged ministers of vengeance, who carry your bolts in their pounces to the remotest verge of the sea. But there a power steps in, that limits the arrogance of raging passions and furious elements, and says, " So far shalt thou go, and no farther." Who are you, that should fret and rage, and bite the chains of nature ?—Nothing worse happens to you than does to all nations who have extensive empire ;

and it happens in all the forms into which empire can be thrown. In large bodies, the circulation of power must be less vigorous at the extremities. Nature has said it. The Turk cannot govern Egypt, and Arabia, and Curdistan, as he governs Thrace ; nor has he the same dominion in Crimea and Algiers, which he has at Brusa and Smyrna. Despotism itself is obliged to truck and huckster. The Sultan gets such obedience as he can. He governs with a loose rein, that he may govern at all ; and the whole of the force and vigour of his authority in his centre is derived from a prudent relaxa- 10 tion in all his borders. Spain, in her provinces, is, perhaps, not so well obeyed as you are in yours. She complies too ; she submits ; she watches times. This is the immutable condition, the eternal law, of extensive and detached empire.

Then, Sir, from these six capital sources ; of descent ; of form of government ; of religion in the northern provinces ; of manners in the southern ; of education ; of the remoteness of situation from the first mover of government ; from all these causes a fierce spirit of liberty has grown up. It has grown 20 with the growth of the people in your colonies, and increased with the increase of their wealth ; a spirit, that unhappily meeting with an exercise of power in England, which, how-ever lawful, is not reconcilable to any ideas of liberty, much less with theirs, has kindled this flame that is ready to con-sume us.

I do not mean to commend either the spirit in this excess, or the moral causes which produce it. Perhaps a more smooth and accommodating spirit of freedom in them would be more acceptable to us. Perhaps ideas of liberty might 30 be desired, more reconcilable with an arbitrary and bound-less authority. Perhaps we might wish the colonists to be persuaded, that their liberty is more secure when held in trust for them by us (as their guardians during a perpetual minority) than with any part of it in their own hands. The question is, not whether their spirit deserves praise or blame,

but—what, in the name of God, shall we do with it? You have before you the object, such as it is, with all its glories, with all its imperfections on its head. You see the magnitude; the importance; the temper; the habits; the disorders. By all these considerations we are strongly urged to determine something concerning it. We are called upon to fix some rule and line for our future conduct, which may give a little stability to our politics, and prevent the return of such unhappy deliberations as the present. Every such
10 return will bring the matter before us in a still more untractable form. For, what astonishing and incredible things have we not seen already! What monsters have not been generated from this unnatural contention! Whilst every principle of authority and resistance has been pushed, upon both sides, as far as it would go, there is nothing so solid and certain, either in reasoning or in practice, that has not been shaken. Until very lately, all authority in America seemed to be nothing but an emanation from yours. Even the popular part of the colony constitution derived all its
20 activity, and its first vital movement, from the pleasure of the crown. We thought, Sir, that the utmost which the discontented colonists could do, was to disturb authority; we never dreamt they could of themselves supply it; knowing in general what an operose business it is to establish a government absolutely new. But having, for our purposes in this contention, resolved, that none but an obedient assembly should sit; the humours of the people there, finding all passage through the legal channels stopped, with great violence broke out another way. Some provinces have
30 tried their experiment, as we have tried ours; and theirs has succeeded. They have formed a government sufficient for its purposes, without the bustle of a revolution, or the troublesome formality of an election. Evident necessity, and tacit consent, have done the business in an instant. So well they have done it, that Lord Dunmore (the account is among the fragments on your table) tells you, that the new institu-

tion is infinitely better obeyed than the ancient government ever was in its most fortunate periods. Obedience is what makes government, and not the names by which it is called ; not the name of governor, as formerly, or committee, as at present. This new government has originated directly from the people ; and was not transmitted through any of the ordinary artificial media of a positive constitution. It was not a manufacture ready formed, and transmitted to them in that condition from England. The evil arising from hence is this ; that the colonists having once found the possibility of 10 enjoying the advantages of order in the midst of a struggle for liberty, such struggles will not henceforward seem so terrible to the settled and sober part of mankind as they had appeared before the trial.

Pursuing the same plan of punishing by the denial of the exercise of government to still greater lengths, we wholly abrogated the ancient government of Massachusetts. We were confident that the first feeling, if not the very prospect of anarchy, would instantly enforce a complete submission. The experiment was tried. A new, strange, unexpected face 20 of things appeared. Anarchy is found tolerable. A vast province has now subsisted, and subsisted in a considerable degree of health and vigour, for near a twelvemonth, without governor, without public council, without judges, without executive magistrates. How long it will continue in this state, or what may arise out of this unheard-of situation, how can the wisest of us conjecture ? Our late experience has taught us that many of those fundamental principles, formerly believed infallible, are either not of the importance they were imagined to be ; or that we have not at all 30 adverted to some other far more important and far more powerful principles, which entirely overrule those we had considered as omnipotent. I am much against any further experiments, which tend to put to the proof any more of these allowed opinions, which contribute so much to the public tranquillity. In effect, we suffer as much at home by

this loosening of all ties, and this concussion of all established
opinions, as we do abroad. For, in order to prove that the
Americans have no right to their liberties, we are every day
endeavouring to subvert the maxims which preserve the
whole spirit of our own. To prove that the Americans
ought not to be free, we are obliged to depreciate the value
of freedom itself; and we never seem to gain a paltry
advantage over them in debate, without attacking some of
those principles, or deriding some of those feelings, for which
10 our ancestors have shed their blood.

But, Sir, in wishing to put an end to pernicious experiments, I do not mean to preclude the fullest inquiry. Far
from it. Far from deciding on a sudden or partial view, I
would patiently go round and round the subject, and survey
it minutely in every possible aspect. Sir, if I were capable
of engaging you to an equal attention, I would state, that, as
far as I am capable of discerning, there are but three ways
of proceeding relative to this stubborn spirit, which prevails
in your colonies, and disturbs your government. These are
20 —To change that spirit, as inconvenient, by removing the
causes. To prosecute it as criminal. Or, to comply with it
as necessary. I would not be guilty of an imperfect enumer-
ation; I can think of but these three. Another has indeed
been started, that of giving up the colonies; but it met so
slight a reception, that I do not think myself obliged to
dwell a great while upon it. It is nothing but a little sally
of anger, like the frowardness of peevish children, who, when
they cannot get all they would have, are resolved to take
nothing.

30 The first of these plans, to change the spirit as inconvenient, by removing the causes, I think is the most like a
systematic proceeding. It is radical in its principle; but it
is attended with great difficulties, some of them little short,
as I conceive, of impossibilities. This will appear by examin-
ing into the plans which have been proposed.

As the growing population in the colonies is evidently one

cause of their resistance, it was last session mentioned in both Houses, by men of weight, and received not without applause, that in order to check this evil, it would be proper for the crown to make no further grants of land. But to this scheme there are two objections. The first, that there is already so much unsettled land in private hands, as to afford room for an immense future population, although the crown not only withheld its grants, but annihilated its soil. If this be the case, then the only effect of this avarice of desolation, this hoarding of a royal wilderness, would be to 10 raise the value of the possessions in the hands of the great private monopolists, without any adequate check to the growing and alarming mischief of population.

But if you stopped your grants, what would be the consequence? The people would occupy without grants. They have already so occupied in many places. You cannot station garrisons in every part of these deserts. If you drive the people from one place, they will carry on their annual tillage, and remove with their flocks and herds to another. Many of the people in the back settlements are already little 20 attached to particular situations. Already they have topped the Appalachian mountains. From thence they behold before them an immense plain, one vast, rich, level meadow; a square of five hundred miles. Over this they would wander without a possibility of restraint; they would change their manners with the habits of their life; would soon forget a government by which they were disowned; would become hordes of English Tartars; and pouring down upon your unfortified frontiers a fierce and irresistible cavalry, become masters of your governors and your counsellors, your collec- 30 tors and comptrollers, and of all the slaves that adhered to them. Such would, and, in no long time, must be, the effect of attempting to forbid as a crime, and to suppress as an evil, the command and blessing of Providence, "Increase and multiply." Such would be the happy result of an endeavour to keep as a lair of wild beasts, that earth, which God, by an

express charter, has given to the children of men.   Far
different, and surely much wiser, has been our policy hitherto.
Hitherto we have invited our people, by every kind of bounty,
to fixed establishments.   We have invited the husbandman
to look to authority for his title.   We have taught him
piously to believe in the mysterious virtue of wax and
parchment.   We have thrown each tract of land, as it was
peopled, into districts ; that the ruling power should never
be wholly out of sight.   We have settled all we could ; and
10 we have carefully attended every settlement with government.

Adhering, Sir, as I do, to this policy, as well as for the
reasons I have just given, I think this new project of
hedging-in population to be neither prudent nor practicable.

To impoverish the colonies in general, and in particular to
arrest the noble course of their marine enterprises, would be
a more easy task.   I freely confess it.   We have shown a
disposition to a system of this kind ; a disposition even to
continue the restraint after the offence ; looking on ourselves
20 as rivals to our colonies, and persuaded that of course we
must gain all that they shall lose.   Much mischief we may
certainly do.   The power inadequate to all other things is
often more than sufficient for this.   I do not look on the
direct and immediate power of the colonies to resist our
violence as very formidable.   In this, however, I may be
mistaken.   But when I consider, that we have colonies for
no purpose but to be serviceable to us, it seems to my
poor understanding a little preposterous, to make them
unserviceable, in order to keep them obedient.   It is, in
30 truth, nothing more than the old, and, as I thought, exploded problem of tyranny, which proposes to beggar its
subjects into submission.   But remember, when you have
completed your system of impoverishment, that nature still
proceeds in her ordinary course; that discontent will increase
with misery ; and that there are critical moments in the
fortune of all states, when they who are too weak to contri-

bute to your prosperity, may be strong enough to complete your ruin. *Spoliatis arma supersunt.* [*The plundered ne'er want arms.*]

The temper and character which prevail in our colonies are, I am afraid, unalterable by any human art. We cannot, I fear, falsify the pedigree of this fierce people, and persuade them that they are not sprung from a nation in whose veins the blood of freedom circulates. The language in which they would hear you tell them this tale would detect the imposition ; your speech would betray you. An Englishman 10 is the unfittest person on earth to argue another Englishman into slavery.

I think it is nearly as little in our power to change their republican religion, as their free descent; or to substitute the Roman Catholic, as a penalty ; or the Church of England, as an improvement. The mode of inquisition and dragooning is going out of fashion in the Old World ; and I should not confide much to their efficacy in the New. The education of the Americans is also on the same unalterable bottom with their religion. You cannot persuade them to 20 burn their books of curious science ; to banish their lawyers from their courts of laws ; or to quench the lights of their assemblies, by refusing to choose those persons who are best read in their privileges. It would be no less impracticable to think of wholly annihilating the popular assemblies, in which these lawyers sit. The army, by which we must govern in their place, would be far more chargeable to us; not quite so effectual ; and perhaps, in the end, full as diffi-cult to be kept in obedience.

With regard to the high aristocratic spirit of Virginia and 30 the southern colonies, it has been proposed, I know, to reduce it, by declaring a general enfranchisement of their slaves. This project has had its advocates and panegyrists ; yet I never could argue myself into any opinion of it. Slaves are often much attached to their masters. A general wild offer of liberty would not always be accepted. History

furnishes few instances of it. It is sometimes as hard to persuade slaves to be free, as it is to compel freemen to be
slaves; and in this auspicious scheme, we should have both
these pleasing tasks on our hands at once. But when we
talk of enfranchisement, do we not perceive that the
American master may enfranchise too; and arm servile
hands in defence of freedom? A measure to which other
people have had recourse more than once, and not without
success, in a desperate situation of their affairs.

10 Slaves as these unfortunate black people are, and dull as
all men are from slavery, must they not a little suspect the
offer of freedom from that very nation which has sold them
to their present masters? from that nation, one of whose
causes of quarrel with those masters is their refusal to deal
any more in that inhuman traffic? An offer of freedom
from England would come rather oddly, shipped to them in
an African vessel, which is refused an entry into the ports of
Virginia or Carolina, with a cargo of three hundred Angola
negroes. It would be curious to see the Guinea captain at-
20 tempting at the same instant to publish his proclamation of
liberty, and to advertise his sale of slaves.

But let us suppose all these moral difficulties got over.
The ocean remains. You cannot pump this dry; and as long
as it continues in its present bed, so long all the causes
which weaken authority by distance will continue. "Ye
gods, annihilate but space and time, and make two lovers
happy!"—was a pious and passionate prayer;—but just as
reasonable, as many of the serious wishes of very grave and
solemn politicians.

30 If then, Sir, it seems almost desperate to think of any alterative course, for changing the moral causes (and not quite easy
to remove the natural) which produce prejudices irreconcil-
able to the late exercise of our authority; but that the spirit
infallibly will continue; and, continuing, will produce such
effects as now embarrass us, the second mode under consideration is, to prosecute that spirit in its overt acts, as *criminal*.

At this proposition I must pause a moment. The thing seems a great deal too big for my ideas of jurisprudence. It should seem to my way of conceiving such matters, that there is a very wide difference in reason and policy, between the mode of proceeding on the irregular conduct of scattered individuals, or even of bands of men, who disturb order within the state, and the civil dissensions which may, from time to time, on great questions, agitate the several communities which compose a great empire. It looks to me to be narrow and pedantic, to apply the ordinary ideas of 10 criminal justice to this great public contest. I do not know the method of drawing up an indictment against a whole people. I cannot insult and ridicule the feelings of millions of my fellow-creatures, as Sir Edward Coke insulted one excellent individual (Sir Walter Raleigh) at the bar. I hope I am not ripe to pass sentence on the gravest public bodies, intrusted with magistracies of great authority and dignity, and charged with the safety of their fellow-citizens, upon the very same title that I am. I really think, that for wise men this is not judicious; for sober men, not decent; 20 for minds tinctured with humanity, not mild and merciful.

Perhaps, Sir, I am mistaken in my idea of an empire, as distinguished from a single state or kingdom. But my idea of it is this; that an empire is the aggregate of many states under one common head; whether this head be a monarch, or a presiding republic. It does, in such constitutions, frequently happen (and nothing but the dismal, cold, dead uniformity of servitude can prevent its happening) that the subordinate parts have many local privileges and immunities. Between these privileges and the supreme common authority 30 the line may be extremely nice. Of course disputes, often, too, very bitter disputes, and much ill blood, will arise. But though every privilege is an exemption (in the case) from the ordinary exercise of the supreme authority, it is no denial of it. The claim of a privilege seems rather, *ex vi termini*, [*by the meaning of the term*] to imply a superior power. For

to talk of the privileges of a state, or of a person, who has no superior, is hardly any better than speaking nonsense. Now, in such unfortunate quarrels among the component parts of a great political union of communities, I can scarcely conceive anything more completely imprudent, than for the head of the empire to insist, that, if any privilege is pleaded against his will, or his acts, his whole authority is denied; instantly to proclaim rebellion, to beat to arms, and to put the offending provinces under the ban. Will not
10 this, Sir, very soon teach the provinces to make no distinctions on their part? Will it not teach them that the government, against which a claim of liberty is tantamount to high treason, is a government to which submission is equivalent to slavery? It may not always be quite convenient to impress dependent communities with such an idea.

We are indeed, in all disputes with the colonies, by the necessity of things, the judge. It is true, Sir. But I confess, that the character of judge in my own cause is a thing
20 that frightens me. Instead of filling me with pride, I am exceedingly humbled by it. I cannot proceed with a stern, assured, judicial confidence, until I find myself in something more like a judicial character. I must have these hesitations as long as I am compelled to recollect, that, in my little reading upon such contests as these, the sense of mankind has, at least, as often decided against the superior as the subordinate power. Sir, let me add too, that the opinion of my having some abstract right in my favour, would not put me much at my ease in passing sentence; unless I could
30 be sure, that there were no rights which, in their exercise under certain circumstances, were not the most odious of all wrongs, and the most vexatious of all injustice. Sir, these considerations have great weight with me, when I find things so circumstanced, that I see the same party, at once a civil litigant against me in point of right, and a culprit before me; while I sit as a criminal judge, on acts of his,

whose moral quality is to be decided upon the merits of that
very litigation.   Men are every now and then put, by the
complexity of human affairs, into strange situations; but
justice is the same, let the judge be in what situation he will.

There is, Sir, also a circumstance which convinces me, that
this mode of criminal proceeding is not (at least in the present stage of our contest) altogether expedient; which is
nothing less than the conduct of those very persons who
have seemed to adopt that mode, by lately declaring a rebellion in Massachusetts Bay, as they had formerly addressed 10
to have traitors brought hither, under an act of Henry the
Eighth, for trial.   For though rebellion is declared, it is not
proceeded against as such; nor have any steps been taken
towards the apprehension or conviction of any individual
offender, either on our late or our former address; but
modes of public coercion have been adopted, and such as
have much more resemblance to a sort of qualified hostility
towards an independent power than the punishment of rebellious subjects.   All this seems rather inconsistent; but it
shows how difficult it is to apply these juridical ideas to our 20
present case.

In this situation, let us seriously and coolly ponder.   What
is it we have got by all our menaces, which have been many
and ferocious?   What advantage have we derived from the
penal laws we have passed, and which, for the time, have
been severe and numerous?   What advances have we made
towards our object, by the sending of a force, which, by land
and sea, is no contemptible strength?   Has the disorder
abated?   Nothing less.—When I see things in this situation, after such confident hopes, bold promises, and active 30
exertions, I cannot, for my life, avoid a suspicion, that the
plan itself is not correctly right.

If then the removal of the causes of this spirit of American
liberty be, for the greater part, or rather entirely, impracticable; if the ideas of criminal process be inapplicable, or if
applicable, are in the highest degree inexpedient; what way

C

yet remains? No way is open, but the third and last—to comply with the American spirit as necessary; or, if you please, to submit to it as a necessary evil.

If we adopt this mode; if we mean to conciliate and concede; let us see of what nature the concession ought to be: to ascertain the nature of our concession, we must look at their complaint. The colonies complain, that they have not the characteristic mark and seal of British freedom. They complain, that they are taxed in a parliament in which they 10 are not represented. If you mean to satisfy them at all, you must satisfy them with regard to this complaint. If you mean to please any people, you must give them the boon which they ask; not what you may think better for them, but of a kind totally different. Such an act may be a wise regulation, but it is no concession: whereas our present theme is the mode of giving satisfaction.

Sir, I think you must perceive, that I am resolved this day to have nothing at all to do with the question of the right of taxation. Some gentlemen startle—but it is true; 20 I put it totally out of the question. It is less than nothing in my consideration. I do not indeed wonder, nor will you, Sir, that gentlemen of profound learning are fond of displaying it on this profound subject. But my consideration is narrow, confined, and wholly limited to the policy of the question. I do not examine, whether the giving away a man's money be a power excepted and reserved out of the general trust of government; and how far all mankind, in all forms of polity, are entitled to an exercise of that right by the charter of nature. Or whether, on the contrary, 30 a right of taxation is necessarily involved in the general principle of legislation, and inseparable from the ordinary supreme power. These are deep questions, where great names militate against each other; where reason is perplexed; and an appeal to authorities only thickens the confusion. For high and reverend authorities lift up their heads on both sides; and there is no sure footing in the middle. This point is the *great Serbonian bog, betwixt Damiata and Mount Casius old, where armies whole have sunk.* I do not intend to be overwhelmed in that bog, though in such respectable company. The question with me is, not whether you have a right to render your people miserable; but whether it is not your interest to make them happy. It is not, what a lawyer tells me I *may* do; but what humanity, reason, and justice tell me I ought to do. Is a politic act the worse for being a generous one? Is no concession proper, but that which is made from your 10 want of right to keep what you grant? Or does it lessen the grace or dignity of relaxing in the exercise of an odious claim, because you have your evidence-room full of titles, and your magazines stuffed with arms to enforce them? What signify all those titles, and all those arms? Of what avail are they, when the reason of the thing tells me, that the assertion of my title is the loss of my suit; and that I could do nothing but wound myself by the use of my own weapons?

Such is stedfastly my opinion of the absolute necessity of 20 keeping up the concord of this empire by a unity of spirit, though in a diversity of operations, that, if I were sure the colonists had, at their leaving this country, sealed a regular compact of servitude; that they had solemnly abjured all the rights of citizens; that they had made a vow to renounce all ideas of liberty for them and their posterity to all generations; yet I should hold myself obliged to conform to the temper I found universally prevalent in my own day, and to govern two millions of men, impatient of servitude, on the principles of freedom. I am not determining a point of law; 30 I am restoring tranquillity; and the general character and situation of a people must determine what sort of government is fitted for them. That point nothing else can or ought to determine.

My idea, therefore, without considering whether we yield as matter of right, or grant as matter of favour, is *to admit*

the people of our colonies into an interest in the constitution;
and, by recording that admission in the journals of parliament, to give them as strong an assurance as the nature of
the thing will admit, that we mean for ever to adhere to
that solemn declaration of systematic indulgence.

Some years ago, the repeal of a revenue act, upon its
understood principle, might have served to show, that we
intended an unconditional abatement of the exercise of a
taxing power. Such a measure was then sufficient to remove
10 all suspicion, and to give perfect content. But unfortunate
events, since that time, may make something further necessary ; and not more necessary for the satisfaction of the
colonies, than for the dignity and consistency of our own
future proceedings.

I have taken a very incorrect measure of the disposition
of the House, if this proposal in itself would be received
with dislike. I think, Sir, we have few American financiers.
But our misfortune is, we are too acute; we are too exquisite
in our conjectures of the future, for men oppressed with
20 such great and present evils. The more moderate among
the opposers of parliamentary concession freely confess, that
they hope no good from taxation ; but they apprehend the
colonists have further views ; and if this point were conceded, they would instantly attack the trade laws. These
gentlemen are convinced, that this was the intention from
the beginning ; and the quarrel of the Americans with taxation was no more than a cloak and cover to this design.
Such has been the language even of a gentleman of real
moderation, and of a natural temper well adjusted to fair
30 and equal government. I am, however, Sir, not a little
surprised at this kind of discourse, whenever I hear it ; and
I am the more surprised, on account of the arguments which
I constantly find in company with it, and which are often
urged from the same mouths, and on the same day.

For instance, when we allege, that it is against reason to tax
a people under so many restraints in trade as the Americans,

the noble lord in the blue riband shall tell you, that the restraints on trade are futile and useless ; of no advantage to us, and of no burthen to those on whom they are imposed; that the trade to America is not secured by the acts of navigation, but by the natural and irresistible advantage of a commercial preference.

Such is the merit of the trade laws in this posture of the debate. But when strong internal circumstances are urged against the taxes ; when the scheme is dissected ; when experience and the nature of things are brought to prove, and 10 do prove, the utter impossibility of obtaining an effective revenue from the colonies; when these things are pressed, or rather press themselves, so as to drive the advocates of colony taxes to a clear admission of the futility of the scheme; then, Sir, the sleeping trade laws revive from their trance ; and this useless taxation is to be kept sacred, not for its own sake, but as a counter-guard and security of the laws of trade.

Then, Sir, you keep up revenue laws which are mischievous, in order to preserve trade laws that are useless. Such is 20 the wisdom of our plan in both its members. They are separately given up as of no value ; and yet one is always to be defended for the sake of the other. But I cannot agree with the noble lord, nor with the pamphlet from whence he seems to have borrowed these ideas, concerning the inutility of the trade laws.   For, without idolizing them, I am sure they are still, in many ways, of great use to us : and in former times they have been of the greatest. They do confine, and they do greatly narrow, the market for the Americans. But my perfect conviction of this does 30 not help me in the least to discern how the revenue laws form any security whatsoever to the commercial regulations ; or that these commercial regulations are the true ground of the quarrel ; or that the giving way, in any one instance of authority, is to lose all that may remain unconceded.

One fact is clear and indisputable. The public and avowed
origin of this quarrel was on taxation. This quarrel has
indeed brought on new disputes on new questions; but
certainly the least bitter, and the fewest of all, on the trade
laws. To judge which of the two be the real, radical cause
of quarrel, we have to see whether the commercial dispute
did, in order of time, precede the dispute on taxation? There
is not a shadow of evidence for it. Next, to enable us to
judge whether at this moment a dislike to the trade laws be
10 the real cause of quarrel, it is absolutely necessary to put
the taxes out of the question by a repeal. See how the
Americans act in this position, and then you will be able to
discern correctly what is the true object of the controversy,
or whether any controversy at all will remain. Unless you
consent to remove this cause of difference, it is impossible,
with decency, to assert that the dispute is not upon what it
is avowed to be. And I would, Sir, recommend to your
serious consideration, whether it be prudent to form a rule
for punishing people, not on their own acts, but on your con-
20 jectures? Surely it is preposterous at the very best. It is
not justifying your anger, by their misconduct; but it is
converting your ill-will into their delinquency.

But the colonies will go further.—Alas! alas! when will
this speculating against fact and reason end?—What will
quiet these panic fears which we entertain of the hostile
effect of a conciliatory conduct? Is it true, that no case
can exist, in which it is proper for the sovereign to accede to
the desires of his discontented subjects? Is there anything
peculiar in this case, to make a rule for itself? Is all
30 authority of course lost, when it is not pushed to the
extreme? Is it a certain maxim, that the fewer causes of
dissatisfaction are left by government, the more the subject
will be inclined to resist and rebel?

All these objections being in fact no more than suspicions,
conjectures, divinations, formed in defiance of fact and
experience; they did not, Sir, discourage me from enter-

taining the idea of a conciliatory concession, founded on the principles which I have just stated.

In forming a plan for this purpose, I endeavoured to put myself in that frame of mind which was the most natural, and the most reasonable ; and which was certainly the most probable means of securing me from all error. I set out with a perfect distrust of my own abilities ; a total renunciation of every speculation of my own ; and with a profound reverence for the wisdom of our ancestors, who have left us the inheritance of so happy a constitution, and so flourishing an 10 empire, and what is a thousand times more valuable, the treasury of the maxims and principles which formed the one, and obtained the other.

During the reigns of the kings of Spain of the Austrian family, whenever they were at a loss in the Spanish councils, it was common for their statesmen to say, that they ought to consult the genius of Philip the Second. The genius of Philip the Second might mislead them ; and the issue of their affairs showed, that they had not chosen the most perfect standard. But, Sir, I am sure that I shall not be 20 misled, when, in a case of constitutional difficulty, I consult the genius of the English constitution. Consulting at that oracle (it was with all due humility and piety) I found four capital examples in a similar case before me ; those of Ireland, Wales, Chester, and Durham.

Ireland, before the English conquest, though never governed by a despotic power, had no parliament. How far the English parliament itself was at that time modelled according to the present form, is disputed among anti-quarians. But we have all the reason in the world to be 30 assured that a form of parliament, such as England then enjoyed, she instantly communicated to Ireland ; and we are equally sure that almost every successive improvement in constitutional liberty, as fast as it was made here, was trans-mitted thither. The feudal baronage, and the feudal knight-hood, the roots of our primitive constitution, were early

transplanted into that soil; and grew and flourished there.
Magna Charta, if it did not give us originally the House of
Commons, gave us at least a House of Commons of weight
and consequence. But your ancestors did not churlishly sit
down alone to the feast of Magna Charta. Ireland was made
immediately a partaker. This benefit of English laws and
liberties, I confess, was not at first extended to *all* Ireland.
Mark the consequence. English authority and English
liberties had exactly the same boundaries. Your standard
10 could never be advanced an inch before your privileges.
Sir John Davis shows beyond a doubt, that the refusal of a
general communication of these rights was the true cause
why Ireland was five hundred years in subduing; and after
the vain projects of a military government, attempted in the
reign of Queen Elizabeth, it was soon discovered, that
nothing could make that country English, in civility and
allegiance, but your laws and your forms of legislature. It
was not English arms, but the English constitution, that
conquered Ireland. From that time, Ireland has ever had a
20 general parliament, as she had before a partial parliament.
You changed the people; you altered the religion; but you
never touched the form or the vital substance of free government in that kingdom. You deposed kings; you restored
them; you altered the succession to theirs, as well as to
your own crown; but you never altered their constitution;
the principle of which was respected by usurpation; restored
with the restoration of monarchy, and established, I trust,
for ever, by the glorious Revolution. This has made Ireland
the great and flourishing kingdom that it is; and from a
30 disgrace and a burthen intolerable to this nation, has
rendered her a principal part of our strength and ornament.
This country cannot be said to have ever formally taxed her.
The irregular things done in the confusion of mighty
troubles, and on the hinge of great revolutions, even if all
were done that is said to have been done, form no example.
If they have any effect in argument, they make an exception

to prove the rule. None of your own liberties could stand a moment if the casual deviations from them, at such times, were suffered to be used as proofs of their nullity. By the lucrative amount of such casual breaches in the constitution, judge what the stated and fixed rule of supply has been in that kingdom. Your Irish pensioners would starve if they had no other fund to live on than taxes granted by English authority. Turn your eyes to those popular grants from whence all your great supplies are come ; and learn to respect that only source of public wealth in the British 10 empire.

My next example is Wales. This country was said to be reduced by Henry the Third. It was said more truly to be so by Edward the First. But though then conquered, it was not looked upon as any part of the realm of England. Its old constitution, whatever that might have been, was destroyed ; and no good one was substituted in its place. The care of that tract was put into the hands of lords marchers—a form of government of a very singular kind ; a strange heterogeneous monster, something between hostility 20 and government ; perhaps it has a sort of resemblance, according to the modes of those times, to that of commander-in-chief at present, to whom all civil power is granted as secondary. The manners of the Welsh nation followed the genius of the government; the people were ferocious, restive, savage, and uncultivated; sometimes composed, never paci-fied. Wales, within itself, was in perpetual disorder ; and it kept the frontier of England in perpetual alarm. Benefits from it to the state there were none. Wales was only known to England by incursion and invasion. 30

Sir, during that state of things, parliament was not idle. They attempted to subdue the fierce spirit of the Welsh by all sorts of rigorous laws. They prohibited by statute the sending all sorts of arms into Wales, as you prohibit by proclamation (with something more of doubt on the legality) the sending arms to America. They disarmed the Welsh by

statute, as you attempted (but still with more question on the legality) to disarm New England by an instruction. They made an act to drag offenders from Wales into England for trial, as you have done (but with more hardship) with regard to America. By another act, where one of the parties was an Englishman, they ordained, that his trial should be always by English. They made acts to restrain trade, as you do; and they prevented the Welsh from the use of fairs and markets, as you do the Americans from fisheries and foreign
10 ports. In short, when the statute book was not quite so much swelled as it is now, you find no less than fifteen acts of penal regulation on the subject of Wales.

Here we rub our hands—A fine body of precedents for the authority of parliament and the use of it!—I admit it fully; and pray add likewise to these precedents, that all the while, Wales rid this kingdom like an *incubus;* that it was an unprofitable and oppressive burthen; and that an Englishman travelling in that country could not go six yards from the high road without being murdered.

20 The march of the human mind is slow. Sir, it was not, until after two hundred years, discovered, that, by an eternal law, Providence had decreed vexation to violence, and poverty to rapine. Your ancestors did however at length open their eyes to the ill husbandry of injustice. They found that the tyranny of a free people could of all tyrannies the least be endured; and that laws made against a whole nation were not the most effectual methods for securing its obedience. Accordingly, in the twenty-seventh year of Henry VIII. the course was entirely altered. With a preamble stating the
30 entire and perfect rights of the crown of England, it gave to the Welsh all the rights and privileges of English subjects. A political order was established; the military power gave way to the civil; the marches were turned into counties. But that a nation should have a right to English liberties, and yet no share at all in the fundamental security of these liberties—the grant of their own property—seemed a thing

so incongruous, that, eight years after, that is, in the thirty-
fifth of that reign, a complete and not ill-proportioned representation by counties and boroughs was bestowed upon
Wales, by act of parliament. From that moment, as by a
charm, the tumults subsided, obedience was restored, peace,
order, and civilization followed in the train of liberty.—
When the day-star of the English constitution had arisen in
their hearts, all was harmony within and without—

> —*Simul alba nautis*
> *Stella refulsit,*   10
> *Defluit saxis agitatus humor;*
> *Concidunt venti, fugiuntque nubes,*
> *Et minax (quod sic voluere) ponto*
> *Unda recumbit.*

> [*Soon as gleam*
> *Their stars at sea,*
> *The lash'd spray trickles from the steep,*
> *The wind sinks down, the storm-cloud flies,*
> *The threatening billow on the deep*
> *Obedient lies.*]   20

The very same year the county palatine of Chester received the same relief from its oppressions, and the same
remedy to its disorders. Before this time Chester was little
less distempered than Wales. The inhabitants, without
rights themselves, were the fittest to destroy the rights of
others; and from thence Richard II. drew the standing
army of archers, with which for a time he oppressed England.
The people of Chester applied to parliament in a petition
penned as I shall read to you:

"To the king our sovereign lord, in most humble wise 30
shown unto your excellent Majesty, the inhabitants of your
Grace's county palatine of Chester; That where the said
county palatine of Chester is and hath been always hitherto
exempt, excluded and separated out and from your high

court of parliament, to have any knights and burgesses
within the said court; by reason whereof the said inhabitants have hitherto sustained manifold disherisons, losses,
and damages, as well in their lands, goods, and bodies, as in
the good, civil, and politic governance and maintenance of
the commonwealth of their said country: (2.) And forasmuch
as the said inhabitants have always hitherto been bound by
the acts and statutes made and ordained by your said High-
ness, and your most noble progenitors, by authority of the
10 said court, as far forth as other counties, cities, and boroughs
have been, that have had their knights and burgesses within
your said court of parliament, and yet have had neither
knight ne burgess there for the said county palatine; the
said inhabitants, for lack thereof, have been oftentimes
touched and grieved with acts and statutes made within
the said court, as well derogatory unto the most ancient
jurisdictions, liberties, and privileges of your said county
palatine, as prejudicial unto the commonwealth, quietness,
rest, and peace of your Grace's most bounden subjects in-
20 habiting within the same."

What did parliament with this audacious address?—Reject
it as a libel? Treat it as an affront to government? Spurn
it as a derogation from the rights of legislature? Did they
toss it over the table? Did they burn it by the hands of the
common hangman? They took the petition of grievance,
all rugged as it was, without softening or temperament,
unpurged of the original bitterness and indignation of complaint; they made it the very preamble to their act of
redress; and consecrated its principle to all ages in the
30 sanctuary of legislation.

Here is my third example. It was attended with the
success of the two former. Chester, civilized as well as
Wales, has demonstrated that freedom, and not servitude, is
the cure of anarchy; as religion, and not atheism, is the true
remedy for superstition. Sir, this pattern of Chester was
followed in the reign of Charles II. with regard to the county

palatine of Durham, which is my fourth example. This county had long lain out of the pale of free legislation. So scrupulously was the example of Chester followed, that the style of the preamble is nearly the same with that of the Chester act; and, without affecting the abstract extent of the authority of parliament, it recognises the equity of not suffering any considerable district, in which the British subjects may act as a body, to be taxed without their own voice in the grant.

Now if the doctrines of policy contained in these preambles, 10 and the force of these examples in the acts of parliament, avail anything, what can be said against applying them with regard to America? Are not the people of America as much Englishmen as the Welsh? The preamble of the act of Henry VIII. says, the Welsh speak a language no way resembling that of his Majesty's English subjects. Are the Americans not as numerous? If we may trust the learned and accurate Judge Barrington's account of North Wales, and take that as a standard to measure the rest, there is no comparison. The people cannot amount to above 200,000; 20 not a tenth part of the number in the colonies. Is America in rebellion? Wales was hardly ever free from it. Have you attempted to govern America by penal statutes? You made fifteen for Wales. But your legislative authority is perfect with regard to America; was it less perfect in Wales, Chester, and Durham? But America is virtually represented. What! does the electric force of virtual representation more easily pass over the Atlantic, than pervade Wales, which lies in your neighbourhood; or than Chester and Durham, surrounded by abundance of representation that is actual 30 and palpable? But, Sir, your ancestors thought this sort of virtual representation, however ample, to be totally insuffi- cient for the freedom of the inhabitants of territories that are so near, and comparatively so inconsiderable. How then can I think it sufficient for those which are infinitely greater, and infinitely more remote?

You will now, Sir, perhaps imagine, that I am on the point of proposing to you a scheme for a representation of the colonies in parliament. Perhaps I might be inclined to entertain some such thought; but a great flood stops me in my course. *Opposuit natura* [*Nature has barred the way*]—I cannot remove the eternal barriers of the creation. The thing, in that mode, I do not know to be possible. As I meddle with no theory, I do not absolutely assert the impracticability of such a representation. But I do not see my way to it; and those who have been more confident have not been more successful. However, the arm of public benevolence is not shortened; and there are often several means to the same end. What nature has disjoined in one way, wisdom may unite in another. When we cannot give the benefit as we would wish, let us not refuse it altogether. If we cannot give the principal, let us find a substitute. But how? Where? What substitute?

Fortunately I am not obliged for the ways and means of this substitute to tax my own unproductive invention. I am not even obliged to go to the rich treasury of the fertile framers of imaginary commonwealths; not to the Republic of Plato; not to the Utopia of More; not to the Oceana of Harrington. It is before me—it is at my feet, *and the rude swain treads daily on it with his clouted shoon.* I only wish you to recognise, for the theory, the ancient constitutional policy of this kingdom with regard to representation, as that policy has been declared in acts of parliament; and, as to the practice, to return to that mode which an uniform experience has marked out to you, as best; and in which you walked with security, advantage, and honour, until the year 1763.

My resolutions therefore mean to establish the equity and justice of a taxation of America, by *grant*, and not by *imposition*. To mark the *legal competency* of the colony assemblies for the support of their government in peace, and for public aids in time of war. To acknowledge that this legal competency has had *a dutiful and beneficial exercise ;* and that experience has shown the *benefit of their grants,* and the *futility of parliamentary taxation as a method of supply.*

These solid truths compose six fundamental propositions. There are three more resolutions corollary to these. If you admit the first set, you can hardly reject the others. But if you admit the first, I shall be far from solicitous whether you accept or refuse the last. I think these six massive pillars will be of strength sufficient to support the temple of British concord. I have no more doubt than I entertain of my existence, that, if you admitted these, you would command an immediate peace ; and, with but tolerable future management, a lasting obedience in America. I am not arrogant in this confident assurance. The propositions are all mere matters of fact ; and if they are such facts as draw irresistible conclusions even in the stating, this is the power of truth, and not any management of mine.

Sir, I shall open the whole plan to you, together with such observations on the motions as may tend to illustrate them where they may want explanation. The first is a resolution —"That the colonies and plantations of Great Britain in North America, consisting of fourteen separate governments, and containing two millions and upwards of free inhabitants, have not had the liberty and privilege of electing and sending any knights and burgesses, or others, to represent them in the high court of parliament."—This is a plain matter of fact, necessary to be laid down, and (excepting the description) it is laid down in the language of the constitution ; it is taken nearly *verbatim* from acts of parliament.

The second is like unto the first—"That the said colonies and plantations have been liable to, and bounden by, several subsidies, payments, rates, and taxes, given and granted by parliament, though the said colonies and plantations have not their knights and burgesses, in the said high court of parliament, of their own election, to represent the condition of their country ; by lack whereof they have been oftentimes

touched and grieved by subsidies given, granted, and assented
to, in the said court, in a manner prejudicial to the commonwealth, quietness, rest, and peace of the subjects inhabiting
within the same."

Is this description too hot, or too cold, too strong, or too
weak? Does it arrogate too much to the supreme legislature? Does it lean too much to the claims of the people?
If it runs into any of these errors, the fault is not mine. It
is the language of your own ancient acts of parliament.

10   *Non meus hic sermo, sed quæ præcepit Ofellus,*
    Rusticus, abnormis sapiens.

        [Ofellus shall set forth
    ('Twas he that taught me it a shrewd clear wit,
    Though country-spun, and for the schools unfit):]

It is the genuine produce of the ancient, rustic, manly, home-
bred sense of this country.—I did not dare to rub off a particle of the venerable rust that rather adorns and preserves,
than destroys, the metal. It would be a profanation to
touch with a tool the stones which construct the sacred altar
20 of peace. I would not violate with modern polish the in-
genuous and noble roughness of these truly constitutional
materials. Above all things, I was resolved not to be guilty
of tampering : the odious vice of restless and unstable minds.
I put my foot in the tracks of our forefathers, where I can
neither wander nor stumble. Determining to fix articles of
peace, I was resolved not to be wise beyond what was written ; I was resolved to use nothing else than the form of
sound words ; to let others abound in their own sense ; and
carefully to abstain from all expressions of my own. What
30 the law has said, I say. In all things else I am silent. I
have no organ but for her words. This, if it be not ingenious, I am sure is safe.

There are indeed words expressive of grievance in this
second resolution, which those who are resolved always to be
in the right will deny to contain matter of fact, as applied to
the present case ; although parliament thought them true,

with regard to the counties of Chester and Durham. They
will deny that the Americans were ever "touched and
grieved" with the taxes. If they consider nothing in taxes
but their weight as pecuniary impositions, there might be
some pretence for this denial. But men may be sorely
touched and deeply grieved in their privileges, as well as in
their purses. Men may lose little in property by the act
which takes away all their freedom. When a man is robbed
of a trifle on the highway, it is not the two-pence lost that
constitutes the capital outrage. This is not confined to 10
privileges. Even ancient indulgences withdrawn, without
offence on the part of those who enjoyed such favours,
operate as grievances. But were the Americans then not
touched and grieved by the taxes, in some measure, merely
as taxes? If so, why were they almost all either wholly repealed or exceedingly reduced? Were they not touched and
grieved even by the regulating duties of the sixth of George
II.? Else why were the duties first reduced to one third in
1764, and afterwards to a third of that third in the year
1766? Were they not touched and grieved by the stamp 20
act? I shall say they were, until that tax is revived.
Were they not touched and grieved by the duties of 1767,
which were likewise repealed, and which Lord Hillsborough
tells you (for the ministry) were laid contrary to the true
principle of commerce? Is not the assurance given by that
noble person to the colonies of a resolution to lay no more
taxes on them, an admission that taxes would touch and
grieve them? Is not the resolution of the noble lord in the
blue riband, now standing on your journals, the strongest of
all proofs that parliamentary subsidies really touched and 30
grieved them? Else why all these changes, modifications,
repeals, assurances, and resolutions?

The next proposition is—"That, from the distance of the
said colonies, and from other circumstances, no method hath
hitherto been devised for procuring a representation in parliament for the said colonies." This is an assertion of a fact.

I go no further on the paper ; though, in my private judgment, an useful representation is impossible ; I am sure it is
not desired by them ; nor ought it perhaps by us ; but I abstain from opinions.

The fourth resolution is—" That each of the said colonies
hath within itself a body, chosen in part, or in the whole, by
the freemen, freeholders, or other free inhabitants thereof,
commonly called the General Assembly, or General Court ;
with powers legally to raise, levy, and assess, according to
10 the several usage of such colonies, duties and taxes towards
defraying all sorts of public services."

This competence in the colony assemblies is certain.   It is
proved by the whole tenor of their acts of supply in all the
assemblies, in which the constant style of granting is, "an
aid to his Majesty ;" and acts granting to the crown have
regularly for near a century passed the public offices without
dispute.   Those who have been pleased paradoxically to deny
this right, holding that none but the British parliament can
grant to the crown, are wished to look to what is done, not
20 only in the colonies, but in Ireland, in one uniform unbroken
tenor every session.   Sir, I am surprised that this doctrine
should come from some of the law servants of the crown.   I
say, that if the crown could be responsible, his Majesty—
but certainly the ministers, and even these law officers themselves, through whose hands the acts pass biennially in Ireland, or annually in the colonies, are in an habitual course of
committing impeachable offences.   What habitual offenders
have been all presidents of the council, all secretaries of
state, all first lords of trade, all attornies and all solicitors
30 general !   However, they are safe ; as no one impeaches
them ; and there is no ground of charge against them, except
in their own unfounded theories.

The fifth resolution is also a resolution of fact—" That the
said general assemblies, general courts, or other bodies
legally qualified as aforesaid, have at sundry times freely
granted several large subsidies and public aids for his

Majesty's service, according to their abilities, when required
thereto by letter from one of his Majesty's principal secretaries of state ; and that their right to grant the same, and
their cheerfulness and sufficiency in the said grants, have
been at sundry times acknowledged by parliament." To say
nothing of their great expenses in the Indian wars ; and
not to take their exertion in foreign ones, so high as the
supplies in the year 1695 ; not to go back to their public
contributions in the year 1710 ; I shall begin to travel only
where the journals give me light ; resolving to deal in 10
nothing but fact, authenticated by parliamentary record ;
and to build myself wholly on that solid basis.

On the 4th of April, 1748, a committee of this House came
to the following resolution :

" Resolved,

" That it is the opinion of this committee, *That it is just
and reasonable* that the several provinces and colonies of
Massachusetts Bay, New Hampshire, Connecticut, and
Rhode Island, be reimbursed the expenses they have been
at in taking and securing to the Crown of Great Britain the 20
island of Cape Breton and its dependencies."

These expenses were immense for such colonies. They
were above £200,000 sterling ; money first raised and advanced on their public credit.

On the 28th of January, 1756, a message from the king
came to us, to this effect :—" His Majesty, being sensible of
the zeal and vigour with which his faithful subjects of
certain colonies in North America have exerted themselves
in defence of his Majesty's just rights and possessions, recommends it to this House to take the same into their con- 30
sideration, and to enable his Majesty to give them such
assistance as may be a *proper reward and encouragement.*"

On the 3rd of February, 1756, the House came to a suitable resolution, expressed in words nearly the same as those
of the message : but with the further addition, that the

money then voted was as an *encouragement* to the colonies to
exert themselves with vigour. It will not be necessary to
go through all the testimonies which your own records have
given to the truth of my resolutions, I will only refer you to
the places in the journals :

Vol. xxvii.—16th and 19th May, 1757.
Vol. xxviii.—June 1st, 1758—April 26th and 30th, 1759
—March 26th and 31st, and April 28th, 1760
—Jan. 9th and 20th, 1761.
10   Vol. xxix.—Jan. 22nd and 26th, 1762—March 14th and
17th, 1763.

Sir, here is the repeated acknowledgment of parliament,
that the colonies not only gave, but gave to satiety. This
nation has formerly acknowledged two things ; first, that the
colonies had gone beyond their abilities, parliament having
thought it necessary to reimburse them ; secondly, that they
had acted legally and laudably in their grants of money, and
their maintenance of troops, since the compensation is expressly given as reward and encouragement. Reward is not
20 bestowed for acts that are unlawful ; and encouragement is
not held out to things that deserve reprehension. My resolution therefore does nothing more than collect into one
proposition, what is scattered through your journals. I give
you nothing but your own ; and you cannot refuse in the
gross, what you have so often acknowledged in detail. The
admission of this, which will be so honourable to them and
to you, will, indeed, be mortal to all the miserable stories, by
which the passions of the misguided people have been engaged in an unhappy system. The people heard, indeed,
30 from the beginning of these disputes, one thing continually
dinned in their ears, that reason and justice demanded, that
the Americans, who paid no taxes, should be compelled to
contribute. How did that fact, of their paying nothing,
stand, when the taxing system began ? When Mr. Grenville
began to form his system of American revenue, he stated in

this House, that the colonies were then in debt two million
six hundred thousand pounds sterling money ; and was of
opinion they would discharge that debt in four years.   On
this state, those untaxed people were actually subject to the
payment of taxes to the amount of six hundred and fifty
thousand a year.   In fact, however, Mr. Grenville was mistaken.   The funds given for sinking the debt did not prove
quite so ample as both the colonies and he expected.   The
calculation was too sanguine ; the reduction was not completed till some years after, and at different times in different 10
colonies.   However, the taxes after the war continued too
great to bear any addition, with prudence or propriety ; and
when the burthens imposed in consequence of former requisitions were discharged, our tone became too high to resort
again to requisition.   No colony, since that time, ever has
had any requisition whatsoever made to it.

We see the sense of the crown, and the sense of parliament, on the productive nature of a *revenue by grant.*   Now
search the same journals for the produce of the *revenue by
imposition*—Where is it ?—let us know the volume and the 20
page—what is the gross, what is the net produce ?—to what
service is it applied ?—how have you appropriated its surplus ?—What, can none of the many skilful index-makers
that we are now employing, find any trace of it ?—Well, let
them and that rest together.—But are the journals, which
say nothing of the revenue, as silent on the discontent ?—
Oh no ! a child may find it.   It is the melancholy burthen
and blot of every page.

I think then I am, from those journals, justified in the
sixth and last resolution, which is—" That it hath been found 30
by experience, that the manner of granting the said supplies
and aids, by the said general assemblies, hath been more
agreeable to the said colonies, and more beneficial, and conducive to the public service, than the mode of giving and
granting aids in parliament, to be raised and paid in the said
colonies."   This makes the whole of the fundamental part

of the plan. The conclusion is irresistible. You cannot say, that you were driven by any necessity to an exercise of the utmost rights of legislature. You cannot assert, that you took on yourselves the task of imposing colony taxes, from the want of another legal body, that is competent to the purpose of supplying the exigencies of the state without wounding the prejudices of the people. Neither is it true that the body so qualified, and having that competence, had neglected the duty.

10 The question now, on all this accumulated matter, is ;— whether you will choose to abide by a profitable experience, or a mischievous theory ; whether you choose to build on imagination, or fact ; whether you prefer enjoyment, or hope ; satisfaction in your subjects, or discontent ?

If these propositions are accepted, everything which has been made to enforce a contrary system, must, I take it for granted, fall along with it. On that ground, I have drawn the following resolution, which, when it comes to be moved, will naturally be divided in a proper manner : " That it may

20 be proper to repeal an act, made in the seventh year of the reign of his present Majesty, intituled, An act for granting certain duties in the British colonies and plantations in America ; for allowing a drawback of the duties of customs upon the exportation from this kingdom, of coffee and cocoa-nuts of the produce of the said colonies or plantations ; for discontinuing the drawbacks payable on China earthenware exported to America ; and for more effectually preventing the clandestine running of goods in the said colonies and plantations.—And that it may be proper to repeal an act,

30 made in the fourteenth year of the reign of his present Majesty, intituled, An act to discontinue, in such manner, and for such time, as are therein mentioned, the landing and discharging, lading or shipping, of goods, wares, and mer-chandise, at the town and within the harbour of Boston, in the province of Massachusetts Bay, in North America.—And that it may be proper to repeal an act, made in the fourteenth

year of the reign of his present Majesty, intituled, An act for
the impartial administration of justice, in the cases of persons
questioned for any acts done by them, in the execution of
the law, or for the suppression of riots and tumults, in the
province of Massachusetts Bay, in New England.—And that
it may be proper to repeal an act, made in the fourteenth
year of the reign of his present Majesty, intituled, An act
for the better regulating the government of the province of
Massachusetts Bay, in New England.—And, also, that it
may be proper to explain and amend an act, made in the 10
thirty-fifth year of the reign of King Henry the Eighth, intituled, An act for the trial of treasons committed out of the
king's dominions."

I wish, Sir, to repeal the Boston Port Bill, because (inde-
pendently of the dangerous precedent of suspending the
rights of the subject during the king's pleasure) it was
passed, as I apprehend, with less regularity, and on more
partial principles, than it ought. The corporation of Boston
was not heard before it was condemned. Other towns, full
as guilty as she was, have not had their ports blocked up. 20
Even the restraining bill of the present session does not go
to the length of the Boston Port Act. The same ideas of
prudence, which induced you not to extend equal punishment to equal guilt, even when you were punishing, induced
me, who mean not to chastise, but to reconcile, to be satisfied
with the punishment already partially inflicted.

Ideas of prudence and accommodation to circumstances,
prevent you from taking away the charters of Connecticut
and Rhode Island, as you have taken away that of Massachusetts colony, though the crown has far less power in the 30
two former provinces than it enjoyed in the latter ; and
though the abuses have been full as great, and as flagrant,
in the exempted as in the punished. The same reasons of
prudence and accommodation have weight with me in restoring the charter of Massachusetts Bay. Besides, Sir, the
act which changes the charter of Massachusetts is in many

particulars so exceptionable, that if I did not wish absolutely
to repeal, I would by all means desire to alter it; as several
of its provisions tend to the subversion of all public and
private justice. Such, among others, is the power in the
governor to change the sheriff at his pleasure; and to make
a new returning officer for every special cause. It is shame-
ful to behold such a regulation standing among English
laws.

The act for bringing persons accused of committing
10 murder under the orders of government to England for
trial is but temporary. That act has calculated the probable duration of our quarrel with the colonies; and is
accommodated to that supposed duration. I would hasten
the happy moment of reconciliation; and therefore must,
on my principle, get rid of that most justly obnoxious act.

The act of Henry the Eighth, for the trial of treasons, I
do not mean to take away, but to confine it to its proper
bounds and original intention; to make it expressly for trial
of treasons (and the greatest treasons may be committed) in
20 places where the jurisdiction of the crown does not extend.

Having guarded the privileges of local legislature, I would
next secure to the colonies a fair and unbiassed judicature;
for which purpose, Sir, I propose the following resolution:
"That, from the time when the general assembly or general
court of any colony or plantation in North America, shall
have appointed by act of assembly, duly confirmed, a settled
salary to the offices of the chief justice and other judges of
the superior court, it may be proper that the said chief justice and other judges of the superior courts of such colony,
30 shall hold his and their office and offices during their good
behaviour; and shall not be removed therefrom, but when
the said removal shall be adjudged by his Majesty in council,
upon a hearing on complaint from the general assembly, or
on a complaint from the governor, or council, or the house of
representatives severally, or of the colony in which the said
chief justice and other judges have exercised the said offices."

The next resolution relates to the courts of admiralty.

It is this :—"That it may be proper to regulate the courts of admiralty, or vice-admiralty, authorized by the fifteenth chapter of the fourth of George the Third, in such a manner as to make the same more commodious to those who sue, or are sued, in the said courts, and to provide for the more decent maintenance of the judges in the same."

These courts I do not wish to take away ; they are in themselves proper establishments. This court is one of the capital securities of the act of navigation. The extent of 10 its jurisdiction, indeed, has been increased ; but this is altogether as proper, and is indeed on many accounts more eligible, where new powers were wanted, than a court absolutely new. But courts incommodiously situated, in effect, deny justice ; and a court, partaking in the fruits of its own condemnation, is a robber. The congress complain, and complain justly, of this grievance.

These are the three consequential propositions. I have thought of two or three more ; but they come rather too near detail, and to the province of executive government ; 20 which I wish parliament always to superintend, never to assume. If the first six are granted, congruity will carry the latter three. If not, the things that remain unrepealed will be, I hope, rather unseemly encumbrances on the building, than very materially detrimental to its strength and stability.

Here, Sir, I should close ; but I plainly perceive some objections remain, which I ought, if possible, to remove. The first will be, that, in resorting to the doctrine of our ancestors, as contained in the preamble to the Chester act, 30 I prove too much ; that the grievance from a want of representation, stated in that preamble, goes to the whole of legislation as well as to taxation. And that the colonies, grounding themselves upon that doctrine, will apply it to all parts of legislative authority.

To this objection, with all possible deference and humility,

and wishing as little as any man living to impair the smallest particle of our supreme authority, I answer, that *the
words are the words of parliament, and not mine;* and, that
all false and inconclusive inferences, drawn from them, are
not mine; for I heartily disclaim any such inference. I
have chosen the words of an act of parliament, which Mr.
Grenville, surely a tolerably zealous and very judicious
advocate for the sovereignty of parliament, formerly moved
to have read at your table in confirmation of his tenets. It
10 is true, that Lord Chatham considered these preambles as
declaring strongly in favour of his opinions. He was a no
less powerful advocate for the privileges of the Americans.
Ought I not from hence to presume, that these preambles
are as favourable as possible to both, when properly understood; favourable both to the rights of parliament, and to
the privilege of the dependencies of this crown? But, Sir,
the object of grievance in my resolution I have not taken
from the Chester, but from the Durham act, which confines
the hardship of want of representation to the case of sub-
20 sidies; and which therefore falls in exactly with the case of
the colonies. But whether the unrepresented counties were
de jure [*in law*], or *de facto* [*in fact*], bound, the preambles
do not accurately distinguish; nor indeed was it necessary;
for, whether *de jure*, or *de facto*, the legislature thought the
exercise of the power of taxing, as of right, or as of fact
without right, equally a grievance, and equally oppressive.

I do not know that the colonies have, in any general way,
or in any cool hour, gone much beyond the demand of im-
munity in relation to taxes. It is not fair to judge of the
30 temper or dispositions of any man, or any set of men, when
they are composed and at rest, from their conduct, or their
expressions, in a state of disturbance and irritation. It is
besides a very great mistake to imagine, that mankind
follow up practically any speculative principle, either of
government or of freedom, as far as it will go in argument
and logical illation. We Englishmen stop very short of the

principles upon which we support any given part of our constitution ; or even the whole of it together. I could easily,
if I had not already tired you, give you very striking and
convincing instances of it. This is nothing but what is
natural and proper. All government, indeed every human
benefit and enjoyment, every virtue, and every prudent act,
is founded on compromise and barter. We balance inconveniences ; we give and take ; we remit some rights that
we may enjoy otheis ; and we choose rather to be happy
citizens than subtle disputants. As we must give away 10
some natural liberty, to enjoy civil advantages ; so we must
sacrifice some civil liberties, for the advantages to be derived
from the communion and fellowship of a great empire. But,
in all fair dealings, the thing bought must bear some proportion to the purchase paid. None will barter away the
immediate jewel of his soul. Though a great house is apt
to make slaves haughty, yet it is purchasing a part of the
artificial importance of a great empire too dear, to pay for it
all essential rights, and all the intrinsic dignity of human
nature. None of us who would not risk his life rather than 20
fall under a government purely arbitrary. But although
there are some amongst us who think our constitution
wants many improvements, to make it a complete system
of liberty ; perhaps none who are of that opinion would
think it right to aim at such improvement, by disturbing
his country, and risking everything that is dear to him. In
every arduous enterprise, we consider what we are to lose as
well as what we are to gain ; and the more and better stake
of liberty every people possess, the less they will hazard in a
vain attempt to make it more. These are *the cords of man*. 30
Man acts from adequate motives relative to his interest ;
and not on metaphysical speculations. Aristotle, the great
master of reasoning, cautions us, and with great weight and
propriety, against this species of delusive geometrical ac-
curacy in moral arguments, as the most fallacious of all
sophistry.

The Americans will have no interest contrary to the grandeur and glory of England, when they are not oppressed by the weight of it; and they will rather be inclined to respect the acts of a superintending legislature, when they see them the acts of that power, which is itself the security, not the rival, of their secondary importance. In this assurance, my mind most perfectly acquiesces: and I confess, I feel not the least alarm from the discontents which are to arise from putting people at their ease; nor do I apprehend
10 the destruction of this empire, from giving, by an act of free grace and indulgence, to two millions of my fellow-citizens some share of those rights, upon which I have always been taught to value myself.

It is said, indeed, that this power of granting, vested in American assemblies, would dissolve the unity of the empire; which was preserved entire, although Wales, and Chester, and Durham were added to it. Truly, Mr. Speaker, I do not know what this unity means; nor has it ever been heard of, that I know, in the constitutional policy of this country.
20 The very idea of subordination of parts, excludes this notion of simple and undivided unity. England is the head; but she is not the head and the members too. Ireland has ever had from the beginning a separate, but not an independent, legislature; which, far from distracting, promoted the union of the whole. Everything was sweetly and harmoniously disposed through both islands for the conservation of English dominion, and the communication of English liberties. I do not see that the same principles might not be carried into twenty islands, and with the same good effect. This is my
30 model with regard to America, as far as the internal circumstances of the two countries are the same. I know no other unity of this empire, than I can draw from its example during these periods, when it seemed to my poor understanding more united than it is now, or than it is likely to be by the present methods.

But since I speak of these methods, I recollect, Mr.

Speaker, almost too late, that I promised, before I finished, to say something of the proposition of the noble lord on the floor, which has been so lately received, and stands on your journals. I must be deeply concerned, whenever it is my misfortune to continue a difference with the majority of this House. But as the reasons for that difference are my apology for thus troubling you, suffer me to state them in a very few words. I shall compress them into as small a body as I possibly can, having already debated that matter at large, when the question was before the committee. 10

First, then, I cannot admit that proposition of a ransom by auction;—because it is a mere project. It is a thing new; unheard of; supported by no experience; justified by no analogy; without example of our ancestors, or root in the constitution.

It is neither regular parliamentary taxation, nor colony grant. *Experimentum in corpore vili* [*Try experiments only upon what is of no value*], is a good rule, which will ever make me adverse to any trial of experiments on what is certainly the most valuable of all subjects, the peace of this 20 empire.

Secondly, it is an experiment which must be fatal in the end to our constitution. For what is it but a scheme for taxing the colonies in the antechamber of the noble lord and his successors? To settle the quotas and proportions in this House, is clearly impossible. You, Sir, may flatter yourself you shall sit a state auctioneer, with your hammer in your hand, and knock down to each colony as it bids. But to settle (on the plan laid down by the noble lord) the true proportional payment for four or five and twenty govern- 30 ments, according to the absolute and the relative wealth of each, and according to the British proportion of wealth and burthen, is a wild and chimerical notion. This new taxation must therefore come in by the back-door of the constitution. Each quota must be brought to this House ready formed; you can neither add nor alter. You must register it. **You** can do nothing further. For on what grounds can you deliberate either before or after the proposition? You cannot hear the counsel for all these provinces, quarrelling each on its own quantity of payment, and its proportion to others. If you should attempt it, the committee of provincial ways and means, or by whatever other name it will delight to be called, must swallow up all the time of parliament.

Thirdly, it does not give satisfaction to the complaint of
10 the colonies. They complain, that they are taxed without their consent ; you answer, that you will fix the sum at which they shall be taxed. That is, you give them the very grievance for the remedy. You tell them indeed, that you will leave the mode to themselves. I really beg pardon : it gives me pain to mention it ; but you must be sensible that you will not perform this part of the compact. For, suppose the colonies were to lay the duties, which furnished their contingent, upon the importation of your manufactures ; you know you would never suffer such a tax to be laid. You
20 know, too, that you would not suffer many other modes of taxation. So that, when you come to explain yourself, it will be found, that you will neither leave to themselves the quantum nor the mode ; nor indeed anything. The whole is delusion from one end to the other.

Fourthly, this method of ransom by auction, unless it be *universally* accepted, will plunge you into great and inextricable difficulties. In what year of our Lord are the proportions of payments to be settled ? To say nothing of the impossibility that colony agents should have general powers
30 of taxing the colonies at their discretion ; consider, I implore you, that the communication by special messages, and orders between these agents and their constituents on each variation of the case, when the parties come to contend together, and to dispute on their relative proportions, will be a matter of delay, perplexity, and confusion that never can have an end.

If all the colonies do not appear at the outcry, what is the condition of those assemblies, who offer by themselves or their agents, to tax themselves up to your ideas of their proportion? The refractory colonies, who refuse all composition, will remain taxed only to your old impositions, which, however grievous in principle, are trifling as to production. The obedient colonies in this scheme are heavily taxed; the refractory remain unburthened. What will you do? Will you lay new and heavier taxes by parliament on the disobedient? Pray consider in what way you can do it. You are perfectly convinced, that, in the way of taxing, you can do nothing but at the ports. Now suppose it is Virginia that refuses to appear at your auction, while Maryland and North Carolina bid handsomely for their ransom, and are taxed to your quota, how will you put these colonies on a par? Will you tax the tobacco of Virginia? If you do, you give its death-wound to your English revenue at home, and to one of the very greatest articles of your own foreign trade. If you tax the import of that rebellious colony, what do you tax but your own manufactures, or the goods of some other obedient and already well-taxed colony? Who has said one word on this labyrinth of detail, which bewilders you more and more as you enter into it? Who has presented, who can present you with a clue, to lead you out of it? I think, Sir, it is impossible, that you should not recollect that the colony bounds are so implicated in one another, (you know it by your other experiments in the bill for prohibiting the New England fishery,) that you can lay no possible restraints on almost any of them which may not be presently eluded, if you do not confound the innocent with the guilty, and burthen those whom, upon every principle, you ought to exonerate. He must be grossly ignorant of America, who thinks that, without falling into this confusion of all rules of equity and policy, you can restrain any single colony, especially Virginia and Maryland, the central and most important of them all.

Let it also be considered, that, either in the present confusion you settle a permanent contingent, which will and
must be trifling; and then you have no effectual revenue:
or you change the quota at every exigency; and then on
every new repartition you will have a new quarrel.

Reflect besides, that when you have fixed a quota for
every colony, you have not provided for prompt and punctual
payment. Suppose one, two, five, ten years' arrears. You
cannot issue a treasury extent against the failing colony.
10 You must make new Boston Port Bills, new restraining laws,
new acts for dragging men to England for trial. You must
send out new fleets, new armies. All is to begin again.
From this day forward the empire is never to know an hour's
tranquillity. An intestine fire will be kept alive in the
bowels of the colonies, which one time or other must con-
sume this whole empire. I allow indeed that the empire of
Germany raises her revenue and her troops by quotas and
contingents; but the revenue of the empire, and the army
of the empire, is the worst revenue and the worst army in
20 the world.

Instead of a standing revenue, you will therefore have a
perpetual quarrel. Indeed the noble lord, who proposed
this project of a ransom by auction, seemed himself to be of
that opinion. His project was rather designed for breaking
the union of the colonies, than for establishing a revenue.
He confessed, he apprehended that his proposal would not
be to *their taste.* I say, this scheme of disunion seems to be
at the bottom of the project; for I will not suspect that the
noble lord meant nothing but merely to delude the nation
30 by an airy phantom which he never intended to realize.
But whatever his views may be; as I propose the peace
and union of the colonies as the very foundation of my plan,
it cannot accord with one whose foundation is perpetual
discord.

Compare the two. This I offer to give you is plain and
simple. The other full of perplexed and intricate mazes.

This is mild; that harsh. This is found by experience
effectual for its purposes; the other is a new project. This
is universal ; the other calculated for certain colonies only.
This is immediate in its conciliatory operation ; the other
remote, contingent, full of hazard. Mine is what becomes
the dignity of a ruling people ; gratuitous, unconditional,
and not held out as matter of bargain and sale. I have done
my duty in proposing it to you. I have indeed tired you by
a long discourse ; but this is the misfortune of those to
whose influence nothing will be conceded, and who must win 10
every inch of their ground by argument. You have heard
me with goodness. May you decide with wisdom ! For my
part, I feel my mind greatly disburthened by what I have
done to-day. I have been the less fearful of trying your
patience, because on this subject I mean to spare it altogether
in future. I have this comfort, that in every stage of the
American affairs, I have steadily opposed the measures that
have produced the confusion, and may bring on the destruction, of this empire. I now go so far as to risk a proposal of
my own. If I cannot give peace to my country, I give it to 20
my conscience.

But what (says the financier) is peace to us without money ?
Your plan gives us no revenue. No ! But it does—For it
secures to the subject the power of REFUSAL ; the first of all
revenues. Experience is a cheat, and fact a liar, if this power
in the subject of proportioning his grant, or of not granting
at all, has not been found the richest mine of revenue ever
discovered by the skill or by the fortune of man. It does not
indeed vote you £152,750 : 11 : 2¾ths, nor any other paltry
limited sum.—But it gives the strong box itself, the fund, the 30
bank, from whence only revenues can arise amongst a people
sensible of freedom : *Posita luditur arca.* [*The chest is
staked.*] Cannot you in England ; cannot you at this time of
day ; cannot you, a House of Commons, trust to the principle
which has raised so mighty a revenue, and accumulated a
debt of near 140 millions in this country ? Is this principle

to be true in England, and false everywhere else ? Is it not true in Ireland ? Has it not hitherto been true in the colonies ? Why should you presume, that, in any country, a body duly constituted for any function, will neglect to perform its duty, and abdicate its trust ? Such a presumption would go against all governments in all modes. But, in truth, this dread of penury of supply, from a free assembly, has no foundation in nature. For first observe, that, besides the desire which all men have naturally of supporting the

10 honour of their own government, that sense of dignity, and that security to property, which ever attends freedom, has a tendency to increase the stock of the free community. Most may be taken where most is accumulated. And what is the soil or climate where experience has not uniformly proved, that the voluntary flow of heaped-up plenty, bursting from the weight of its own rich luxuriance, has ever run with a more copious stream of revenue, than could be squeezed from the dry husks of oppressed indigence, by the straining of all the politic machinery in the world.

20 Next we know, that parties must ever exist in a free country. We know too, that the emulations of such parties, their contradictions, their reciprocal necessities, their hopes, and their fears, must send them all in their turns to him that holds the balance of the state. The parties are the gamesters ; but government keeps the table, and is sure to be the winner in the end. When this game is played, I really think it is more to be feared that the people will be exhausted, than that government will not be supplied. Whereas, whatever is got by acts of absolute power ill obeyed, because

30 odious, or by contracts ill kept, because constrained, will be narrow, feeble, uncertain, and precarious. *" Ease would retract vows made in pain, as violent and void."*

I, for one, protest against compounding our demands : I declare against compounding for a poor limited sum, the immense, evergrowing, eternal debt, which is due to generous government from protected freedom. And so may I speed in the great object I propose to you, as I think it would not only be an act of injustice, but would be the worst economy in the world, to compel the colonies to a sum certain, either in the way of ransom, or in the way of compulsory compact.

But to clear up my ideas on this subject—a revenue from America transmitted hither—do not delude yourselves—you never can receive it—No, not a shilling. We have experience that from remote countries it is not to be expected. If, when you attempted to extract revenue from Bengal, you were obliged to return in loan what you had taken in imposition ; 10 what can you expect from North America ? For certainly, if ever there was a country qualified to produce wealth, it is India ; or an institution fit for the transmission, it is the East India Company. America has none of these aptitudes. If America gives you taxable objects, on which you lay your duties here, and gives you, at the same time, a surplus by a foreign sale of her commodities to pay the duties on these objects, which you tax at home, she has performed her part to the British revenue. But with regard to her own internal establishments ; she may, I doubt not she will, contribute in 20 moderation. I say in moderation ; for she ought not to be permitted to exhaust herself. She ought to be reserved to a war ; the weight of which, with the enemies that we are most likely to have, must be considerable in her quarter of the globe. There she may serve you, and serve you essentially.

For that service, for all service, whether of revenue, trade, or empire, my trust is in her interest in the British constitution. My hold of the colonies is in the close affection which grows from common names, from kindred blood, from 30 similar privileges, and equal protection. These are ties, which, though light as air, are as strong as links of iron. Let the colonies always keep the idea of their civil rights associated with your government ;—they will cling and grapple to you ; and no force under heaven will be of power to tear them from their allegiance. But let it be once under-

stood, that your government may be one thing, and their
privileges another ; that these two things may exist without
any mutual relation ; the cement is gone ; the cohesion is
loosened ; and everything hastens to decay and dissolution.
As long as you have the wisdom to keep the sovereign
authority of this country as the sanctuary of liberty, the
sacred temple consecrated to our common faith, wherever the
chosen race and sons of England worship freedom, they will
turn their faces towards you. The more they multiply, the
10 more friends you will have ; the more ardently they love
liberty, the more perfect will be their obedience. Slavery
they can have anywhere. It is a weed that grows in every
soil. They may have it from Spain, they may have it from
Prussia. But, until you become lost to all feeling of your
true interest and your natural dignity, freedom they can
have from none but you. This is the commodity of price, of
which you have the monopoly. This is the true act of navigation, which binds to you the commerce of the colonies, and
through them secures to you the wealth of the world. Deny
20 them this participation of freedom, and you break that sole
bond, which originally made, and must still preserve, the
unity of the empire. Do not entertain so weak an imagination, as that your registers and your bonds, your affidavits
and your sufferances, your cockets and your clearances, are
what form the great securities of your commerce. Do not
dream that your letters of office, and your instructions, and
your suspending clauses, are the things that hold together
the great contexture of the mysterious whole. These things
do not make your government. Dead instruments, passive
30 tools as they are, it is the spirit of the English communion
that gives all their life and efficacy to them. It is the spirit
of the English constitution, which, infused through the
mighty mass, pervades, feeds, unites, invigorates, vivifies
every part of the empire, even down to the minutest member.

Is it not the same virtue which does everything for us
here in England ? Do you imagine then, that it is the land

tax act which raises your revenue ? that it is the annual vote
in the committee of supply which gives you your army ? or
that it is the mutiny bill which inspires it with bravery and
discipline ? No ! surely no ! It is the love of the people ; it
is their attachment to their government, from the sense of
the deep stake they have in such a glorious institution, which
gives you your army and your navy, and infuses into both
that liberal obedience, without which your army would be a
base rabble, and your navy nothing but rotten timber.

All this, I know well enough, will sound wild and chimeri- 10
cal to the profane herd of those vulgar and mechanical politicians, who have no place among us ; a sort of people who
think that nothing exists but what is gross and material ;
and who therefore, far from being qualified to be directors
of the great movement of empire, are not fit to turn a wheel
in the machine. But to men truly initiated and rightly
taught, these ruling and master principles, which, in the
opinion of such men as I have mentioned, have no substantial
existence, are in truth everything, and all in all. Magnanimity in politics is not seldom the truest wisdom ; and a 20
great empire and little minds go ill together. If we are
conscious of our situation, and glow with zeal to fill our place
as becomes our station and ourselves, we ought to auspicate
all our public proceedings on America with the old warning
of the church, *Sursum corda !* [*Lift up your hearts.*] We
ought to elevate our minds to the greatness of that trust to
which the order of Providence has called us. By adverting
to the dignity of this high calling, our ancestors have turned
a savage wilderness into a glorious empire ; and have made
the most extensive, and the only honourable conquests, not 30
by destroying, but by promoting the wealth, the number,
the happiness of the human race. Let us get an American
revenue as we have got an American empire. English privileges have made it all that it is ; English privileges alone
will make it all it can be.

In full confidence of this unalterable truth, I now (*quod*

felix faustumque sit) [*and may it be lucky and fortunate*] **lay**
the first stone of the temple of peace ; and I move you,

"That the colonies and plantations of Great Britain in
North America, consisting of fourteen separate governments,
and containing two millions and upwards of free inhabitants,
have not had the liberty and privilege of electing and
sending any knights and burgesses, or others, to represent
them in the high court of parliament."

Upon this resolution, the previous question was put, and
10 carried ;—for the previous question 270, against it 78.   The
second, third, fourth, and thirteenth resolutions had also the
previous question put on them.   The others were negatived.

Mr. Burke's Proposals.

"That the colonies and plantations of Great Britain in
North America, consisting of fourteen separate governments,
and containing two millions and upwards of free inhabitants,
have not had the liberty and privilege of electing and sending
any knights and burgesses, or others, to represent them in
the high court of parliament."
20   "That the said colonies and plantations have been made
liable to, and bounden by, several subsidies, payments, rates,
and taxes, given and granted by parliament ; though the said
colonies and plantations have not their knights and burgesses,
in the said high court of parliament, of their own election, to
represent the condition of their country ; by lack whereof
they have been oftentimes touched and grieved by subsidies
given, granted, and assented to, in the said court, in a manner
prejudicial to the commonwealth, quietness, rest, and peace,
of the subjects inhabiting within the same."
30   "That, from the distance of the said colonies, and from
other circumstances, no method hath hitherto been devised
for procuring a representation in parliament for the said
colonies."

"That each of the said colonies hath within itself a body, chosen, in part or in the whole, by the freemen, freeholders, or other free inhabitants thereof, commonly called the general assembly, or general court; with powers legally to raise, levy, and assess, according to the several usage of such colonies, duties and taxes towards defraying all sorts of public services."

"That the said general assemblies, general courts, or other bodies, legally qualified as aforesaid, have at sundry times freely granted several large subsidies and public aids for his 10 Majesty's service, according to their abilities, when required thereto by letter from one of his Majesty's principal secretaries of state ; and that their right to grant the same, and their cheerfulness and sufficiency in the said grants, have been at sundry times acknowledged by parliament."

"That it hath been found by experience, that the manner of granting the said supplies and aids, by the said general assemblies, hath been more agreeable to the inhabitants of the said colonies, and more beneficial and conducive to the public service, than the mode of giving and granting aids and 20 subsidies in parliament to be raised and paid in the said colonies."

"That it may be proper to repeal an act, made in the seventh year of the reign of his present Majesty, intituled, An act for granting certain duties in the British colonies and plantations in America ; for allowing a drawback of the duties of customs, upon the exportation from this kingdom, of coffee and cocoa-nuts, of the produce of the said colonies or plantations ; for discontinuing the drawbacks payable on China earthenware exported to America ; and for more 30 effectually preventing the clandestine running of goods in the said colonies and plantations."

"That it may be proper to repeal an act, made in the fourteenth year of the reign of his present Majesty, intituled, An act to discontinue, in such manner, and for such time, as are therein mentioned, the landing and discharging, lading or shipping of goods, wares, and merchandise, at the town, and within the harbour, of Boston, in the province of Massachusetts Bay, in North America."

"That it may be proper to repeal an act, made in the fourteenth year of the reign of his present Majesty, intituled, An act for the impartial administration of justice, in cases of persons questioned for any acts done by them in the execution of the law, or for the suppression of riots and tumults, in the province of Massachusetts Bay, in New England."

10 "That it is proper to repeal an act, made in the fourteenth year of the reign of his present Majesty, intituled, An act for the better regulating the government of the province of Massachusetts Bay, in New England."

"That it is proper to explain and amend an act made in the thirty-fifth year of the reign of King Henry VIII., intituled, An act for the trial of treasons committed out of the king's dominions."

"That, from the time when the general assembly, or general court, of any colony or plantation, in North America, 20 shall have appointed, by act of assembly duly confirmed, a settled salary to the offices of the chief justice and judges of the superior courts, it may be proper that the said chief justice and other judges of the superior courts of such colony shall hold his and their office and offices during their good behaviour; and shall not be removed therefrom, but when the said removal shall be adjudged by his Majesty in council, upon a hearing on complaint from the general assembly, or on a complaint from the governor, or council, or the house of representatives, severally, of the colony in which the said 30 chief justice and other judges have exercised the said office."

"That it may be proper to regulate the courts of admiralty, or vice-admiralty, authorized by the fifteenth chapter of the fourth of George III., in such a manner, as to make the same more commodious to those who sue, or are sued, in the said courts; and to provide for the more decent maintenance of the judges of the same."

NOTES

SPEECH ON CONCILIATION WITH AMERICA.

P. 2, l. 1. **the Chair,** the position which you occupy as president of this House. The strictness and severity which the Speaker has to exercise in the maintenance of order are supposed to have rendered him impatient of human weaknesses.

l. 4. **depending,** hanging over them, imminent. When a man is very anxious, the slightest circumstance is sufficient to encourage or to depress him.

l. 7. **the event,** the result.

l. 8. **the grand penal bill,** the object of which was to restrict the trade of the New England colonies with Great Britain, Ireland, and the British Islands in the West Indies, and also to prevent them, except under certain conditions and limitations, from carrying on their fisheries in Newfoundland. To destroy the trade of the Americans was to deprive them of the means of subsistence.

l. 10. **is to be returned,** etc., the Lords returned it to the Commons for reconsideration. They thought that its provisions might be extended to other colonies.

l. 13. **we are put once more,** etc. The House of Commons has finally committed itself to a bill which it has once sent up to the Lords. In this case, Burke says, God Himself seems to have intervened to prevent the disastrous results of the bill, by giving the Commons an opportunity of reconsidering it.

l. 21. **coercion and restraint,** by the *coercion* he means the attempt to break the American resistance to the tea-duty : by the *restraint*, the limitation placed on their trade. These two things were different, but hardly incongruous.

P. 3, l. 5. **When I first,** etc. In 1765, when Burke sat as member for the borough of Wendover.

l. 7. **delicate,** requiring careful handling.

l. 10. **trust,** Burke often insists that the power of a government is not absolute, but given to it only to be exercised for the good of the people and the empire. The interests of the nation are committed to its charge, as the property of a ward is to a trustee. This view, which is essentially Whig, is emphasized by Locke, who traces the origin of government back to a contract entered into by peoples to make a conditional surrender of some of their natural rights to government with a view to better securing the rest.

l. 12. **I was obliged,** etc. Burke probably knew more about America than any one in England.

l. 19. **to ballast,** to steady. *Ballast* means, literally, a weight put in a ship to steady it. A man who has fixed opinions of his own is not shaken by the changes in popular sentiment and opinion. **blown about,** etc. The language throughout is in harmony with the comparison of the steadiness given to him by fixed opinions and the steadiness given to a ship by ballast. He did not profess whatever was the opinion of the majority for the moment. The words are borrowed from St. Paul, *Eph.* iv. 14, "That we henceforth be no more children, tossed to and fro, and carried about with every wind of doctrine, by the sleight of men, and cunning craftiness, whereby they lie in wait to deceive."

l. 21. **manly,** A man should be strong, and able to rely on his own resources. Burke was ready with a standard by which to judge of any events that might be reported from America. It was just because Burke did look at events in the light of consistent principles that his works have value. His position must be the position of any man who aspires to what can be called an opinion on political matters.

l. 23. **At that period,** etc. It was the time of the repeal of the Stamp Act.

l. 29. **religious,** scrupulous.

l. 30. **it is in,** etc. I leave it to your fairness to decide.

l. 31. **Parliament having,** etc. A change in feeling and conduct can only be justified by a change in circumstances. Parliament knows more of circumstances than an individual can do, and may therefore reasonably change more frequently than a private individual.

P. 4, l. 1. **to,** joined with motives: their reasons for their many changes in feeling and policy.

l. 4. **complaint,** Used in its common meaning of a *disease.*

l. 5. **the distemper,** disorder, derangement, disease.

l. 8. **I will not miscall,** etc. My regard for truth will not allow me to represent the evil as being less than it really is. It is so appalling that I am afraid to call it by its proper name, even if I could find a name adequate to describe it.

l. 11. **a worthy member,** Mr. Rose Fuller.

l. 12. **filled the chair,** etc., presided when the affairs of America were being considered in Committee of the whole House.

l. 15. **our former methods,** viz., criticism of government measures.

l. 17. **never too indulgent,** etc., an unsuccessful opposition is apt to be regarded by public opinion as factious.

l. 21. **inconstancy,** levity, want of fixed principle. As the Ministry proposed measures of every kind, and the Opposition objected to all of them, it might seem as if they had made up their minds beforehand not to be contented with anything that came from the Government. To this, of course, Burke would reply that he criticised the Government because they wavered between conciliation and coercion, instead of sticking consistently to one of them.

l. 26. **out,** to the end.

l. 27. **our hand,** literally, the cards in our hand, that is to say, our own policy. The word, of course, is used because the struggle between the Government and the Opposition has just been compared to a game at cards.

l. 31. **a platform,** a ground plan. They would be expected to give at least an outline of their own scheme.

l. 35. **His application,** his request for a scheme of government.

P. 5, l. 1. **No man,** etc. No one could be more willing than myself, because no one could be more anxious than I was for the welfare of America ; but it was not for a private individual like myself to frame a scheme of government, because I should have no power to give effect to it when it was framed.

l. 2. **gave ... into,** yielded to.

l. 5. **argues,** is a sign of the existence of, proves.

l. 9. **disreputably,** to the damage of the reputation of. The word now carries the sense of positive disgrace.

l. 13. **I have,** etc. As a rule I have a very poor opinion of mere schemes of government, and of any measure which is not to be enforced by the man who drafts it. When a man knows that he is to be practically responsible for carrying out a measure which he devises, he will, for his own sake, carefully inform himself as to all the circumstances of the country to which it is to be applied, and will propose nothing that does not appear to be really practicable. A private individual, drawing up a scheme of government, does so under no sense of responsibility.

l. 18. **alienation,** estrangement.

l. 19. **I felt this**, etc. When the safety of a country is at stake, it is the duty of private individuals to come forward and give what help they can. Cf. "If the prudence of reserve and decorum dictate silence in some cases, in others prudence of an higher order may justify us in speaking our thoughts" (*Reflections on the Revolution in France*).

l. 21. **is a mighty leveller**, equalizes all, that is, in times of danger all may help.

l. 27. **would ennoble**, etc. The loftiest efforts of genius would be dignified by the cause in which they were made ; and every man would be justified in doing his best, no matter how little it might be, to help in such a crisis.

l. 32. **I grew less anxious**, Because as he goes on to explain, he knew that his proposal would be judged on its merits.

P. 6, l. 1. **natural or adventitious.** *Natural* describes the influence which a man possesses owing to his own intrinsic worth : *adventitious* describes that which *comes to* a man from external circumstances, such as his rank or office.

l. 8. **the labyrinth**, a maze. The expression shows the difficulty of arriving at an agreement by negotiation.

l. 9. **to arise**, etc. Burke is perhaps thinking of the Roman principle of ruling by creating divisions amongst the ruled.

l. 11. **not peace**, etc. I do not wish peace to depend on the answer which a lawyer may give to such a difficult question as "What does sovereignty include?"

l. 13. **shadowy**, obscure, hard to discern. Burke is, of course, referring to the question which had been raised as to the extent of England's rights in the matter of taxation.

l. 14. **in its ordinary haunts**, literally in the places which it ordinarily frequents. To seek it in such places means 'to take the right way of getting it.' If you have quarrelled with a man and want to make friends with him again, you must show your anxiety to do so by removing the cause of offence. Then he will meet you half way.

l. 17. **former unsuspecting**, etc. These words are in italics because they were used by the congress at Philadelphia to describe the state of feeling in America after the repeal of the Stamp Act. Burke refers to them again in the letter to the sheriffs of Bristol.

l. 23. **Refined**, opposed to simple.

l. 25. **Plain good intention**, etc. If you want your subjects to obey you, let them see that you really mean them well.

l. 28. **healing**, It puts an end to discord, which is the disease of the state.

l. 29. **cementing,** It binds the parts of the empire together, as mortar binds bricks.

l. 32. **pruriency,** literally, itching ; and so curiosity, or inquisitiveness. It is always used in a bad sense, signifying generally a desire to hear something improper or indelicate.

l. 34. **the project,** "That when the Governor, Council, or Assembly, or general Court, of any of his Majesty's provinces or colonies in America shall *propose* to make provision, *according to the condition, circumstances,* and *situation* of such province or colony, for contributing their *proportion* to the *common defence* (such proportion to be raised under the authority of the general Court, or general Assembly, of such province or colony, and disposable by parliament), and shall engage to make provision also for the support of the civil government, and the administration of justice, in such province or colony, it will be proper, *if such proposal shall be approved by his Majesty, and the two Houses of Parliament,* and for so long as such provision shall be made accordingly, to forbear, *in respect of such province or colony,* to levy any duty, tax, or assessment, or to impose any further duty, tax, or assessment, except such duties as it may be expedient to continue to levy or impose for the regulation of commerce ; the nett produce of the duties last mentioned to be carried to the account of such province or colony respectively" (Resolution moved by Lord North in the committee, and agreed to by the House, 27th February, 1775).

l. 35. **the blue riband,** the badge of the Order of the Garter. It is very seldom that a Commoner is a Knight of the Garter. Lord North sat in the House of Commons because he was only the second son of the Earl of Guildford, and the younger sons of peers, even when they bear courtesy titles, are, for all legal and political purposes, commoners. Scotch and Irish peers are also found in the House of Commons, because only sixteen Scotch, and eight Irish peers are entitled to sit in the House of Lords. The Scotch peers are elected, at the opening of a new Parliament, by an assembly of peers at Holyrood. The Irish peers are elected for life.

l. 36. **your lobby,** the anteroom of the House. Only members are allowed within the actual precincts of the House : **squabbling,** disputing as to the amount which each colony should pay. Every agent will try to make out that his own colony should pay least.

P. 7, l. 1. **your mace,** the Serjeant-at-Arms, who is the executive officer of the House of Commons. The mace is the sign of his authority.

l. 3. **auction of finance,** Just as people bid for articles at an auction, so the colonies would make a bid for exemption from taxation by the British Parliament.

l. 4. **come to general ransom**, free themselves from taxation by a voluntary payment. To ransom means to redeem, or buy off.

l. 5. **knock down the hammer**, accept the contribution offered by them. When at an auction no one will go beyond the last offer, or bid, the auctioneer, saying 'Going, going, going—gone,' brings his hammer down on the table and declares that article sold.

l. 6. **beyond all the powers**, etc. No amount of knowledge of the science of calculating could enable a man to decide the fair contribution for each of a number of colonies so differently situated. Cf. p. 61, l. 25.

l. 9. **the proposition and registry**, its having been brought forward and recorded in your journals.

l. 13. **menacing front**, its threatening appearance. The House had promised to aid the Crown in putting down the rebellion in Massachusetts. **Our address:** The address is the reply of Parliament to the speech from the throne, or declaration of ministerial policy, with which Parliament opens. It is moved and seconded by two supporters of Government. Amendments may be proposed to it, and the debate on the address is made an occasion for challenging the policy of Government or the conduct of particular ministers. **our heavy bills**, etc., referring to the closing of Boston harbour and the suspension of colonial assemblies.

l. 18. **It has even**, etc., it has gone further ; it has done more than this.

P. 8, l. 4. **either in effect**, etc., it is not lessened, nor is it thought to be lessened.

l. 11. **are the strength**, etc. The only chance which the weaker party has of treating on equal terms with the stronger is to catch the latter at a disadvantage.

l. 22. **the object**, America. Burke's meaning is this—America is too valuable a possession for us to run any risk of losing it. It is too powerful a country for us to have any chance of subduing it.

P. 9, l. 9. **shoots**, a word used to describe the growth of a tree.

l. 16. **from families**, etc., perhaps a reminiscence of Aristotle. He said, and truly, that the social unit is the family. Families form village communities, and these communities are consolidated into states. Athens arose out of a union into one political organization of a number of village communities.

l. 19. **in the front of**, etc. I mention it first. I give it the most prominent place.

l. 21. **pinched**, confined : meagre.

l. 22. **occasional system,** It is of no use applying a system adapted to the circumstances of to-day to a country in which circumstances, *e.g.* the number of inhabitants, are changing.

l. 23. **one of those minima,** it is not one of those insignificant objects which we can afford to neglect. Burke is alluding to the maxim, *De minimis non curat lex, i.e.* there are trifles of which law takes no account.

l. 31. **without guilt,** it must always be wrong wantonly to offend and damage numbers of men. The Americans will resist any attempt which you make to harm them.

P. 10, l. 1. **This ground ... has been trod,** This subject has been dealt with.

l. 3. **at your bar,** The bar is a rod drawn across the entry to the chamber in which Parliament sits, and to which members only are admitted. Witnesses, giving evidence before the House, have to stand behind this bar.

l. 4. **This gentleman,** Mr. Glover. The planters of the West Indies petitioned the House of Commons to make peace with the colonies, supporting their petition by pointing out how they would suffer if the Americans carried out their resolution to import nothing from English territories. **after thirty-five years,** his former appearance was probably connected with the matters that led to the war of England with Spain in 1739. Spain tried to prevent England from trading with Spanish America.

l. 9. **the first literary characters,** Glover's epics, *Leonidas* and the *Atheniad,* and his tragedies, *Boadicea* and *Medea,* are now forgotten.

l. 10. **in,** with regard to.

l. 21. **state,** statement.

l. 27. **vouchers,** authorities. To vouch is the Latin *vocare, to call* as evidence.

l. 28. **on your table,** presented officially to the House.

l. 30. **office,** viz., of customs.

l. 33. **terminating almost wholly,** etc. Our trade with Africa must be reckoned as a part of our colonial trade ; because with what we export to Africa we buy African slaves, which are then sent on and sold in the colonies. The English trade with Africa was really a slave trade with the colonies.

P. 11, l. 3. **denominations,** trades nominally distinct.

P. 12, l. 6. **protuberance,** etc., has not our increased trade with America been purchased at the cost of our trade with other countries ? Have we not spent so much in America that we have nothing left to spend in other countries ? *A protuberance* means, literally, a bulging or swelling. The killing of one trade by another is compared to the death of a man from a tumour, which absorbs the juices that ought to go to sustain the rest of his body.

l. 8. **It is the very food,** The profits of our American trade have enabled us to produce more, to sell more, and therefore to buy more, than we could before.

l. 20. **sophistical,** false. The Sophists were teachers who appeared in Greece in the fourth century B.C. They professed to teach the accomplishments, specially rhetoric, which were required for practical success in a democratic city. They were distrusted by orthodox conservatives as men who taught 'the art of making the worst cause seem the better.' Plato and Aristotle are specially responsible for the evil connotation which attaches to the words *sophist* and *sophistry.* They regarded the Sophists as vendors of spurious knowledge. Burke means that an object of so much value must be dealt with carefully.

l. 22. **It is good,** etc., it is well that we should dwell upon it. "And after six days Jesus taketh with him Peter, and James, and John, and leadeth them up into an high mountain apart by themselves: and he was transfigured before them. And his raiment became shining, exceeding white as snow; so as no fuller on earth can white them. And there appeared unto them Elias with Moses: and they were talking with Jesus. And Peter answered and said to Jesus, master, *it is good for us to be here*" (*Mark*, ix. 2-5).

l. 31. **of an age,** he was born in 1684. The quotation which follows is slightly altered from Virgil, *Eclogue*, iv. 26.

l. 35. **the angel,** the belief that a guardian spirit is commissioned by the Deity to watch over every man from life to death was very ancient and widespread. The Romans called this guardian spirit a man's *Genius.* Hence the use of the word in p. 13, l. 14. **auspicious,** favoured, fortunate. The word *auspice* means lit. an omen taken from the flight of birds.

P. 13, l. 2. **fourth generation ... third prince,** George III. was the grandson of George II.

l. 5. **healing counsels,** because they put an end to the discords between England and Scotland. **was to be made Great Britain,** referring to the Act of Union between England and Scotland in 1707.

l. 6. **he should see his son.** His son was made Lord Chancellor with the title of Baron Apsley in 1771.

l. 7. **turn back the current,** etc., the sovereign is the fountain of honour. In the ordinary course honours derived from him descend from father to son. In this case the ordinary course was reversed. The son received a barony in his father's lifetime, and the father was raised to an earldom. This reversal of the ordinary course is compared by Burke to a stream flowing back to its source.

l. 16. **seminal principle**, compared to America, as it was in Burke's day, it was then what a seed is to a tree. *Semen* is the Latin for *seed*.

l. 20. **you taste of death**, "Verily I say unto you, There be some standing here that shall not *taste of death*, till they see the Son of Man coming in his kingdom" (*Matt.* xvi. 28).

l. 31. **the setting of his day**, the closing years of his life.

P. 14, l. 10. **to sink it**, to convey an inadequate idea of it. Very large figures only convey a very vague impression.

l. 16. **deceive the burthen**, lighten it, make men forget it. The Latin word for to deceive, *fallere*, is used in this sense.

l. 17. **invigorate the springs**, etc. We receive from America the materials for manufactured goods, which we sell either in England or abroad.

l. 25. **comprehending**, including.

l. 31. **child of your old age**, the colonies are the children of the mother-country. They are the children of her old age, because it was not until after many years of England's existence that Englishmen settled in America.

l. 32. **piety**, used like the Lat. *pietas*, to signify the affection which binds a child to its father : **a Roman charity**, Roman writers tell how one Cimon was condemned to death by starvation in prison. His daughter Xanthippe was allowed to visit him, and she kept her father alive by feeding him with the milk from her own breast.

P. 15, l. 8. **tumbling mountains**, etc., icebergs. The word *berg* is the German word for a mountain.

l. 13. **the frozen serpent**, a small constellation within the Antarctic circle.

l. 15. **romantic**, fanciful. It was so remote that the acquisition of it by any nation seemed a dream. But though other nations could not go so far, the Americans have gone beyond it. The Falkland Islands are S.E. of South America. The student will find an account of them in Mahon's *Hist. of England*, vol. v. ch. 49. The word romance is used to denote any story of love or adventure, because such stories were frequent in the literature of those languages of South Europe which were derived from the language of Rome.

l. 16. **a stage and resting-place**, like an inn on a journey.

l. 19. **draw the line**, etc. The harpoon, or spear with which the whale is wounded, is fastened to a rope which is wound round a tub in the whaling-boat. When the whale is struck, the unwinding of the rope allows him to go clear of the boat, which he would otherwise upset.

l. 20. **run the longitude,** sail southwards.

l. 21. **game,** the word is applied to all creatures that are hunted.

l. 22. **No sea but what,** etc., there is no sea which is not harassed by them. Burke had in mind similar uses of the word *vexare* by Latin poets—Lucretius, *e.g.* talks of mountains being *vexed* by the wind.

l. 26. **hardy,** bold, adventurous.

l. 28. **in the gristle,** only half developed. Gristle is connected with to grind, because it has to be crunched with the teeth if eaten.

l. 34. **generous,** The word means literally of noble birth, and so comes to denote the qualities which a man of noble birth ought to possess.

P. 16, l. 3. **My rigour,** etc. No government, however watchful or however careful, could have produced these results. When I think of this I feel no disposition to put any checks upon freedom. Seeing what good it can do, I am willing to pardon the occasional evils for which it is responsible.

l. 8. **Certainly it is,** etc. Notice the skill with which Burke refutes an argument by putting it in a way that exposes the folly of it.

l. 11. **complexions,** characters. The word complexion, which we now use to describe the appearance of the face, formerly signified either character or physical constitution.

l. 13. **Those who wield,** etc., the government who dispose of the forces of the state.

l. 25. **Terror is not,** etc. You must not take it for granted that the Americans will be intimidated by your threats, or that your forces will necessarily be victorious.

l. 32. **you impair,** you diminish the value of. Life and money must be expended in war.

P. 17, l. 3. **a foreign enemy.** France would have been glad to find England at a disadvantage.

l. 5. **no insurance,** I cannot guarantee myself. The word *sure* is the same as *secure, i.e.* free from anxiety.

l. 9. **no sort of experience,** This argument is characteristic of Burke.

l. 14. **our fault,** what my opponents represent as the mistake of over-indulgence. By **our penitence** he means our policy of coercion.

l. 27. **as an ardent**, etc.   Our hatred of those who would rob us of a thing is great in proportion to the value which we set upon the thing.

l. 28. **restive**, restless, disturbed.   The word properly means stubborn, unwilling to move : but it is confused with the word restless : **untractable**, unmanageable.

l. 30. **shuffle ... by chicane**, to get from them by underhand measures.

P. 18, l. 2. **England**, etc.   In his speech on American taxation Burke indicated his opinion that the English did not guard their freedom as watchfully as their ancestors did ; and in the *Present Discontents* he reproves them for sitting quietly by while the Court perverted the popular house into an instrument of despotism.

l. 4. **when this part**, etc., when England was struggling for freedom under the Stuarts.   The Puritan emigrants wanted freedom to worship according to their conscience.

l. 5. **bias**, literally, a slant ; and so, an inclination to one side, in this case to the side of, or in the direction of, freedom.

l. 8. **English ideas**, etc., as Englishmen understand it, viz., a freedom to dispose of their own money ; and as Englishmen justify it, viz., on the ground that a man who can be robbed of his money is not free.   **Abstract liberty**, liberty in general, *i.e.* mere absence of control.   There is no country in which every one may do whatever he likes.

l. 9. **Liberty inheres**, etc.   Freedom is freedom in some particular respect, or freedom to do some particular thing.

l. 11. **by way of eminence**, especially, pre-eminently.   Burke's words are a translation of the Greek phrase, κατ' ἐξοχήν.   We generally use the French phrase, *par excellence*.

l. 15. **the ancient commonwealths**, Rome and the states in Greece.   Every student will remember the struggles between the patricians and plebeians in Rome, and between the oligarchical and democratic factions in Greece.

l. 22. **to give ... satisfaction**, to demonstrate.

l. 27. **parchments**, charters.   The word is derived from Pergamus, a town in Asia Minor, where parchment was first invented : **blind**, for which no good reason could be given.

l. 32. **the old records**, the parchments referred to above.

l. 33. **This oracle**, this truth.   The word oracle means, literally, an utterance of the deity.

l. 35. **mediately or immediately**, by themselves or their representatives.   They not only showed, as a matter of history, that the sovereign had not taxed ; but they also argued *a priori*, or deductively, that a people, whom a sovereign could deprive of their money at his pleasure, could not be free.

P. 19, l. 3. **fixed and attached,** used intransitively.

l. 4. **Liberty might be,** etc. Burke means that men count themselves free when they are free to do the particular things that they care about doing.

l. 6. **Here they felt,** etc. Just as a doctor, when he wants to find out whether a man is healthy (sound) or not, feels his pulse, so the Americans, when they wished to know whether they were free or not, asked whether they were taxed by themselves or by England.

l. 10. **It is not easy,** etc. You must not expect to keep your principles and all that follows from them to yourselves. If you proclaim that only those who are self-taxed are free, why should this be true of Englishmen in England only ?

l. 12. **and your mode,** etc. By granting them practical freedom, *i.e.* by the policy of non-interference which you have adopted, you have strengthened their belief in their freedom.

l. 16. **They were further,** etc. If they were not to be free, why did you give them the free institutions of England ? **pleasing error,** they were pleased with the belief in their own freedom, but it now appears as if that belief was an illusion.

l. 18. **merely popular,** altogether popular. Merely is used in its literal sense of purely. *Merus* is the Latin word for *unmixed.* Burke means to say that in every colony there was a popular assembly, summoned by the Governor, but that in *New England* the colonies were pure democracies. In Massachusetts the Upper Chamber, instead of being, as in most provinces, appointed by the Sovereign, was elected annually by the Lower Chamber : every town officer was annually chosen ; all town affairs were decided in public meetings ; the clergy were selected by their congregations ; and with the exception of a few custom house officers, the Crown officers were paid by the State. The Governor was appointed by the Crown, but his power was practically very limited, because his salary and the salaries of the whole Executive depended on the popular vote. In Rhode Island and Connecticut the freemen elected all their officers from the highest to the lowest, and they were not obliged to communicate the acts of their local legislatures to the king (Lecky).

l. 24. **this necessary operation,** the inevitable tendency of free institutions to produce a spirit of independence in those who live under them.

l. 26. **a principle of energy,** an active principle. A man will do and suffer for his religion, if it is sincere.

l. 29. **of that kind,** viz., dissenters from the Church of England. The term dissenters is applied to all religious sects among Englishmen outside the Established Church.

l. 32. **built upon it,** because, unless every man is free to
worship God in his own way, the existence of independent
religious sects is unjustifiable.

l. 33. **from,** this is the right preposition to use after **averse** (cf.
above, l. 22), though now we generally use *to*.

l. 35. **in their history,** Their dislike of absolute governments
is due to the fact that they or their ancestors were oppressed by
absolute governments.

l. 36. **coeval with,** as old as.

P. 20, l. 3. **The Church of England,** etc. It was established by
Henry VIII.

l. 8. **natural liberty,** a natural liberty is one which is not
created by and cannot be taken away by government. The expression *state of nature* is used to denote the period anterior to
the existence of society and governments ; and natural liberties
are the rights which men were supposed to have enjoyed in that
period. The claim of the secular government to repress dissent
can only be resisted on the ground that the right of every man
to worship as he pleases is a right which he possessed before the
existence of governments, and which, therefore, no government
can abrogate.

l. 10. **cold and passive,** lukewarm and indifferent. A Protestant must be a man who protests against something or some-
body.

l. 12. **is a refinement,** etc., it is the right to protest and dissent carried to its extreme limits. It is Protestantism and
dissent in its extreme form. Englishmen in the 16th century
asserted their right to protest against the Romish corruptions of
primitive belief and worship. Dissenters assert the right to
differ from any church, and to protest against any belief or
practice whatsoever.

l. 15. **denominations,** the regular word used to denote a religious
sect : **agreeing in nothing,** etc. No two sects have exactly the
same creed or form of worship ; but they all agree in this, that
any man may believe what he pleases, and worship as he pleases.

l. 20. **left England,** during the struggle with the Stuarts.

l. 24. **the establishments,** the technical word for State churches.
Cf. below, l. 30. There were in America Irish Presbyterians,
besides Germans, Swedes, Scotch, Welsh, and a few Dutch
immigrants (Lecky).

l. 25. **far from alien to,** very much akin to.

l. 28. **the latitude,** etc., they think that I am asserting of all
America what is only true of a part of it. If we attribute the
spirit of independence to the prevalence of dissent, how are we
to account for it where dissent is not prevalent ? Burke says that

though the Southerners are not dissenters, they are slave owners, and the ownership of slaves produces the same haughty spirit in them that dissent does in the Northerners.

l. 30. **has a regular establishment,** In Virginia " the sixty or seventy clergymen of the Established Church received, in addition to a house and to some glebe lands, an annual stipend in the form of tobacco, which was delivered to them packed in hogsheads for exportation at the nearest warehouse " (Lecky).

P. 21, l. 1. **jealous of their freedom,** Seeing as they do every day the superiority of their own position as freemen to that of their slaves, the value of freedom is constantly forced upon their attention. They naturally cling to their freedom when they have before their eyes every day examples of the misery of the non-free.

l. 4. **a common blessing,** enjoyed by all. The words which follow "as broad ... air," are from *Macbeth*, iii. 4. 23. In a free country many of the poorer class seem little better than slaves. They have to work as hard, if they can get work, and they are not so well housed nor so well fed. Freedom does not seem worth so much in a country where free men may be wretched.

l. 10. **I cannot alter,** etc. Burke wanted the English to realize that they had to deal with America as it was. What was the use of arguing that the spirit of independence in the Americans of the Southern colonies, being simply a feeling of pride arising out of a comparison between themselves and their dependents, had nothing in it that deserved respect ? The question was not what made them independent, but was there any chance that an independent people would submit tamely to an arbitrary government ?

l. 14. **ancient commonwealths,** slavery prevailed in Rome and in all the states of Greece : **Gothic ancestors,** Burke uses the word Gothic loosely as equivalent to *German.* Goths is properly the name of a single Teutonic people who inhabited the Southern shores and the islands of the Baltic.

l. 15. **in our days,** we need not go to ancient history for a parallel. We have seen one in our own days. In Poland the peasants were serfs attached to the soil. Burke uses the past tense *were,* because the position of the peasantry was much improved upon the partition of Poland in 1772 between Russia, Prussia, and Austria.

l. 17. **domination,** the word is appropriate, because *dominus* was the Latin term for an owner or master of slaves.

l. 23. **The profession,** the actual lawyers.

l. 25. **the congress,** viz., at Philadelphia. See Introduction.

l. 28. **tracts,** treatises. It is a short form of tractate. The word is specially applied to short publications on religious subjects.

l. 32. **Blackstone's Commentaries,** Blackstone was born in 1723. He wrote the famous *Commentaries on the Laws of England,* a book which has profoundly influenced the opinions of English-men upon the subject of the English law and constitution.

P. 22, l. 1. **chicane,** a trick or subterfuge.

l. 2. **your capital,** etc., your chief punitive measures. Burke refers to the prohibition of public meetings. The people evaded the act, by calling every meeting an adjournment of a meeting held before the act was passed. **The smartness of debate will say,** Some clever man among my opponents will reply that the study of the law must teach them to respect the law.

l. 5. **All this is mighty well,** It is easy enough to say this, but plausible as it sounds, every one knows that there is nothing in it.

l. 6. **friend on the floor,** the Attorney-General Thurlow. The benches in the House of Commons rise in tiers : the lowest bench to the right of the Speaker is occupied by the members of the Government, the corresponding bench on his left being reserved for the leaders of the Opposition. Thurlow was making notes of points in Burke's speech to be replied to.

l. 7. **animadversion,** means lit. attention or notice; but gener-ally signifies censure.

l. 10. **this knowledge,** the knowledge of law. The way to stop the criticism of a lawyer is to give him a good appointment. Every Indian student will appreciate the truth of Burke's remarks about lawyers.

l. 13. **Abeunt studia,** etc., Ovid, *Heroid.* xv. 83. Cf. "His-tories make men wise : poets witty : the mathematics subtle : natural philosophy deep : morals grave : logic and rhetoric able to contend. *Abeunt studia in mores*" (Bacon, *Essay* 50); and "It is not without truth which is said, that studies have an influence and operation upon the manners of those that are con-versant in them " (*Advancement of Learning,* bk. i.).

l. 16. **of a less mercurial cast,** of a less lively temperament, more stolid. Mercurial means, literally, like quicksilver : **judge of an ill principle,** only decide that there is something amiss in the Government when they have actually begun to suffer.

l. 18. **judge of the pressure,** They do not say that a policy is bad because it is oppressive, but that it must be oppressive because it is bad.

l. 19. **They augur,** etc., they can see it coming. The Latin noun augur (properly *avigur,* from *avis,* a bird) signified one who foretold the future from observation of the flight of birds.

l. 20. **and snuff**, etc., just as the dog's sense of smell enables him to detect the presence of an animal before he sees it, so the ingenuity of these men enables them to anticipate the measures of Government before they are passed. *Snuff,* scent. *Tainted,* viz., by the smell of the animal.

l. 23. **it is not merely moral**, etc., it is not a matter affecting character, but is an unalterable physical circumstance.

l. 29. **You have, indeed**, etc., it is true that you have ships which can carry your forces to the most distant parts of the earth. The ships carrying troops are compared to birds carrying thunder-bolts in their talons (pounces) with reference to the eagle who, in the Roman mythology, had charge of the thunderbolts of the god Jupiter.

l. 33. **So far**, etc., referring to the story of Canute ordering the flow of the tide to cease. Burke means that England could not possibly conquer the Americans in a war carried on on the American continent.

l. 34. **Who are you**, etc. In what are you superior to other men that you should expect nature to remove obstacles for you alone? The metaphor is from a horse champing his bit.

P. 23, l. 1. **in all the forms**, whether the imperial power be a despotism, or a constitutional monarchy, or a republic.

l. 2. **In large bodies**, etc., in large empires, the power of the central government must be weak in the distant provinces. The metaphor is from the circulation of the blood. Burke's statement requires qualification. It is contradicted by the strength of the British Government in distant lands. Much less depends on distance than on the character of the ruling government.

l. 3. **Nature has said it**, it is an unalterable law.

l. 5. **Crimea and Algiers**, Algiers is the capital of Algeria, a district on the north coast of Africa, which since 1830 has been under French rule. The Crimea, a peninsula of S. Russia, has been in the hands of Russia since 1757. Brusa and Smyrna are on the coast of Turkey in Asia.

l. 6. **Despotism itself**, etc. Even a ruler with absolute power, and much more a Government like yours, is obliged to higgle and bargain with his subjects as to the amount of obedience he is to get from them. Burke is thinking of a bargain between a hawker and his customers. The hawker does not get all he asks, but all he can. Similarly, the Government does not get as much obedience as it would like, but as much as it can. **To truck** means, literally, to barter or exchange. **Huckster** is the same word as hawker, and means, literally, to stoop under a burden. The hawker carries his pack on his back.

l. 8. **with a loose rein,** like a driver who allows his horse to go his own pace.

l. 10. **in his centre,** at home. If he dispersed his forces throughout his empire, he would not have the means of enforcing his authority at home.

l. 11. **Spain,** etc. You have nothing to complain of. You are as well obeyed as other imperial powers, if not better.

l. 16. **capital,** chief. They are descended from Englishmen; their government is popular; they are dissenters in the North; they are slave owners in the South; they study law and are far from England.

l. 19. **the first mover,** Burke probably had in his mind the *primum mobile* of the Ptolemaic astronomy. The heavenly bodies, it was thought, were set in a series of spheres, having the earth as their common centre. The outermost of these spheres was called the 'primum mobile' or 'first moved.' It completed its revolution in twenty-four hours, and communicated its movement to the inner spheres. Bacon similarly compares the sovereign to the *primum mobile*, Essay xv., "The motions of the greatest persons in a government ought to be as the motions of the planets under *primum mobile* (according to the old opinion), which is, that every one of them is carried swiftly by the highest motion, and softly in their own motion."

l. 24. **much less with theirs,** because, as already explained, what they understand by freedom is freedom from arbitrary taxation. 'A consuming fire' is a Biblical expression.

l. 27. **I do not mean,** etc., the question is not whether the American character is admirable or not, but how the Americans, their character being what it is, are to be dealt with. Nobody doubts that the task of governing them would be easier if they were less independent.

l. 29. **smooth,** unresisting. **accommodating,** ready to meet our wishes.

l. 30. **Perhaps ideas,** etc., it would be pleasanter for us if they could think themselves free, though arbitrarily taxed.

l. 33. **held in trust,** etc., as property is held by a guardian for his ward so long as the ward is under age.

P. 24, l. 1. **in the name of God,** the words show how serious the question is.

l. 3. **with all its imperfections,** etc. Hamlet's father relating the circumstances of his death tells how he was

> "Cut off even in the blossoms of my sin,
> Unhousel'd, disappointed, unaneled,
> No reckoning made, but sent to my account
> With all my imperfections on my head" (*Haml.* i. 5. 79).

l. 6. **to determine something,** Similarly in his speech on American taxation Burke said, 'Let us, Sir, embrace some system or other before we end this session.'

l. 9. **Every such,** etc., because the discontent of the Americans was naturally increasing.

l. 12. **monsters,** prodigies. He is referring, as he goes on to explain, to the upsettal of long accepted opinions.

l. 13. **unnatural,** the quarrel between England and her colonies was like a quarrel between parent and child.

l. 16. **reasoning,** theory.

l. 19. **the popular part,** the representative assemblies. They were summoned by the Governors, who were nominated by the Crown.

l. 24. **operose,** laborious.

l. 28. **finding all passage,** etc., being unable to give expression to their grievances through their assemblies, because these assemblies were suspended.

l. 33. **Evident necessity,** etc., the whole population have quietly acquiesced in arrangements which they saw to be necessary.

l. 35. **Lord Dunmore,** Governor of Virginia.

P. 25, l. 2. **Obedience,** etc., the real government is the body which is obeyed.

l. 7. **artificial media,** such, for instance, as royal charters or Acts of Parliament: **positive,** as opposed to *natural,* signifies anything which is accepted by convention. The English constitution is positive in the sense that it is the one under which the English have agreed to live. There was nothing to prevent them from choosing a different one if they had liked; nor is there any reason in the nature of things why it should be accepted out of England.

l. 9. **The evil,** etc. Here again the student will notice how Burke sees the permanent lessons taught by events.

l. 18. **feeling,** actual experience.

l. 28. **fundamental principles,** such, for instance, as the importance of government to general well-being.

l. 33. **I am much against,** etc. This sentence is very characteristic of Burke. He was so impressed with the value of social order and with the difficulty of creating it, that he shrank from any attack upon opinions, feelings, or even prejudices that in any way tended to maintain it. When he considered how naturally lawless, selfish, passionate, and violent man is, the mere existence of society seemed to him, literally, *a mystery.*

P. 26, l. 1. **concussion,** shaking.

l. 2. **For, in order,** etc. This is very important. The policy pursued towards America was only a part of the general system of arbitrary government to which Burke, in his *Present Discontents*, had traced the existing discontent in England. Those who favoured despotism in America could not logically object to it when they themselves were made the object of it. If sovereignty as such includes the right to tax, it must do so in England, as well as in America. If the Americans were not justified in defending their freedom, England would not be justified in defending the very same freedom against the Crown.

l. 9. **for which our ancestors,** etc. So in his speech on American taxation Burke said, "The feelings of the Colonies were formerly the feelings of Great Britain. Theirs were formerly the feelings of Mr. Hampden when called upon for the payment of twenty shillings. Would twenty shillings have ruined Mr. Hampden's fortune? No! but the payment of half twenty shillings, on the principle it was demanded, would have made him a slave."

l. 24. **giving up the colonies,** Tucker, Dean of Gloucester, an extreme Tory, had advocated the cession of the Colonies on the ground that they were a source of weakness to England, and that, so far as the profits of trade were concerned, even if America were made independent, the cheap markets of England would still attract American buyers.

l. 26. **sally,** an outburst. It is generally applied to a sudden rush of a besieged garrison upon its besiegers.

l. 32. **It is radical,** etc., it goes *to the root* of the matter.

P. 27, l. 6. **unsettled,** as yet unoccupied.

l. 10. **hoarding,** to hoard means to keep wealth unemployed: **royal,** because the land belonged to the sovereign.

l. 12. **private monopolists,** individuals to whom grants had been made, as distinguished from the *royal* monopolist, viz., the king. If the king refused to make further grants of waste land, the individuals to whom such land had already been granted would, of course, have a monopoly of it. They alone would have it to let or to sell, consequently they could ask their own price for it.

l. 18. **they will carry on,** etc., they would become nomads. Burke probably had in mind a passage in Horace, in which the words *annual tillage* occur.

"Happier the Scythians, wont o'er townless wilds
 To shift the wains that are their nomad dwellings:
Or the rude Getae whose unmeted soil
 Yields its free sheaves and fruits to all in common;
Thus each man toils but for his single year," etc.
                    (*Od.* iii. 24. 9, Martin's Translation).

l. 20. **back settlements**, those in the interior.

l. 28. **hordes**, from *úrdú*, the Tartar word for a royal camp. They would degenerate into barbarians, and would overrun civilized America, just as the Asiatic tribe of Tartars had, at times, overrun and wasted, for instance, the eastern parts of Europe, and the northern parts of India. The name *Tartar* should be spelt *Tatar*. The *r* was introduced to make their name describe them. They were regarded as fiends from Tartarus, the Greek word for *hell*.

l. 31. **comptrollers**, another spelling of *controller*, control being short for counter-roll. A controller is one who keeps a duplicate register by which to verify the original.

l. 34. **blessing**, the word signifies any gift, favour, or privilege conferred by God. " So God created man in his own image, in the image of God created he him ; male and female created he them. And God *blessed* them, and God said unto them, *Be fruit-ful and multiply*, and replenish the earth, and subdue it," etc. (*Genesis*, i. 27). Burke, as Mr. Payne points out, took the form " *Encrease* and multiply " from Milton (*P. L.* x. 730). Milton translated from the Vulgate, or Latin Bible.

P. 28, l. 1. **given to the children of men**, " The heaven, even the heavens, are the Lord's : but the earth hath he given to the children of men" (*Psalm*, cxv. 16). Cf. Locke's *Treatise* of *Government*, bk. ii. ch. 5.

l. 5. **his title**, his right to his land.

l. 6. **wax and parchment**, legal documents, contracts. Deeds of sale, etc., are written on parchment, because of its durability, and are sealed with wax. Burke means that we have taught men to regard contracts as sacred. The result of the policy which Burke condemns would be to imbue men with the belief that " those may take who have the power, and those may keep who can." At the bottom of all Burke's thoughts about com-munities and governments there lay a certain mysticism. It was no irony, no literary trope, when he talked of our having taught the American husbandman " piously to believe in the mysterious virtue of wax and parchment." He was using no idle epithet when he described the disposition of a stupendous wisdom, " moulding together the great mysterious incorporation of the human race." To him there actually was an element of mystery in the cohesion of men in societies, in political obedience, in the sanctity of contract, in all that fabric of law and charter and obligation, whether written or unwritten, which is the sheltering bulwark between civilization and barbarism. When reason and history had contributed all that they could to the explanation, it seemed to him as if the vital force, the secret of organization, the binding framework, must still come from the impenetrable regions beyond reasoning and beyond history (Lord Morley). See note on p. 25, l. 33.

l. 14. **hedging-in,** confining.

l. 16. **their marine enterprises,** their fisheries, of which Burke has already given so eloquent a description.

l. 20. **we must gain,** etc. It was a common fallacy that every restriction on the trade of one country must mean a corresponding gain to the trade of another country. Bacon says that "whatsoever is somewhere gotten must be somewhere lost." The right of England to control American trade being allowed, it was, as Burke says, easy for them to punish America by imposing restrictions. The restrictions were often continued after the occasion for them had been removed under the idea that England gained by them. It was forgotten that a country can only buy with what it makes. To diminish American trade, therefore, was to diminish America's power of buying English goods.

l. 24. **direct and immediate,** etc. But the colonies would probably find allies amongst England's enemies.

l. 27. **to my poor understanding,** in my humble opinion. There is a very effective irony in this affected apology for what is plain common sense.

l. 31. **exploded,** rejected : obsolete. The word signified in Latin "to drive a play off the stage by a noisy clapping of hands." Tyrants attempt to enforce obedience by taking away the means of resistance.

P. 29, l. 2. **Spoliatis,** etc. From the Roman satirist Juvenal (*Satire,* viii. 124).

l. 10. **your speech would betray you,** Your common language would betray your common origin. When Jesus was put on His trial before the Jewish high priest, Caiaphas, Peter, one of His disciples, attempted to disavow any connection with Him, "and after a while came unto him they that stood by, and said to Peter, Surely thou also art one of them : for *thy speech bewrayeth thee*" (*Matt.* xxvi. 73).

l. 11. **is the unfittest person,** etc., because he is so perfectly free himself.

l. 15. **as a penalty,** This is said from the point of view of a member of the English Church.

l. 16. **The mode of inquisition,** etc. It is no longer possible, as it once was, to frighten heretics by the penalties of spiritual courts or the employment of military force. The *inquisition* was

a Catholic Court for the trial of heretics. It was formally constituted in the middle of the thirteenth century. *Dragoon* signified originally a cavalry soldier armed with an infantry firearm,
and trained to fight on foot as well as on horseback. The name
was derived from the dragon's head worked upon the muzzles of
the short muskets first carried by Marshal Brissac's horsemen in
the year 1600 (Chambers). "In 1535 an Imperial Edict was
issued in Brussels condemning all heretics to death ; repentant
males to be executed with the sword, repentant females to be
buried alive, the obstinate of both sexes to be burned" (Motley's
Dutch Republic). Students will remember Milton's sonnet on
the massacre of the Protestants in Piedmont in 1655.

l. 20. **bottom,** basis, foundation. It is equally unalterable.

l. 21. **their books of curious science,** their law books. In the
Acts of the Apostles, xix. 19, where a victory of the Christian
Apostle Paul over some Jewish exorcists is described, it is said
that "many of them also which used curious arts brought their
books together, and burned them before all men." *Curious*
means magical.

l. 23. **best read in,** best acquainted with, through their study
of Acts of Parliament, etc.

l. 27. **chargeable,** costly ; literally, burdensome.

l. 28. **difficult to be kept,** etc. Cf. "Fierce licentiousness
begets violent restraints. The military arm is the sole reliance;
and then, call your constitution what you please, it is the sword
that governs. The civil power, like every other that calls in the
aid of an ally stronger than itself, perishes by the assistance it
receives " (*Present Discontents*).

l. 30. **high aristocratic spirit,** the pride which comes of a sense
of superiority. The word aristocracy means, literally, government by the best, that is, by the wisest and most virtuous. It
acquired its present sense of a government of wealth and rank
because the rich and the noble naturally arrogate to themselves
the title of the best.

l. 31. **to reduce it,** to bring it down, to lower it.

l. 33. **panegyrists,** eulogists. The Greek word *panegyris*
meant a public assembly ; and a *panegyric* is a complimentary
speech such as would be delivered in a public assembly. Dunmore,
in Virginia, had proclaimed "freedom to all indented servants,
negroes, or others, appertaining to rebels," if they would "join
for the reducing of the colony to a proper sense of its duty "
(Bancroft, vol. vii.).

l. 34. **argue myself,** etc. See any reasons for entertaining a
favourable opinion of it.

l. 36. **wild,** made without reflection. "To the African negroes
bondage in Virginia was not a lower condition of being than their
former one; they had no regrets for ancient privileges lost; their
memories prompted no demand for political change; no struggling
aspirations of their own had invited Dunmore's interposition; no
memorial of their grievances had preceded his offers" (Bancroft).

P. 30, l. 3. **auspicious,** see on p. 12, l. 35. It is ironical.
both these pleasing tasks, the task of compelling the slaves to
accept freedom, and of compelling the Americans to submit to
despotic rule.

l. 7. **other people,** Greek states and the Romans sometimes did
this, when the citizen population was not sufficiently numerous
to cope with a national enemy.

l. 10. **dull,** stupid. Long years of cruelty alone produce intel-
lectual torpor, but, besides this, there is nothing to stimulate
the ingenuity of a slave. However skilful his work might be, it
would bring no advantages to himself.

l. 12. **that very nation,** England. As the slaves knew that
England forced them upon the Americans, they would not look
upon an offer of freedom from England as disinterested.

l. 15. **An offer of freedom,** etc. What will the slaves think of
an offer of freedom forwarded to them by the same English ship
which carries a cargo of fresh slaves whom the Americans are
unwilling to buy? Angola is on the west coast of Africa.

l. 19. **the Guinea captain,** the captain of a ship which sailed
from Guinea with a cargo of slaves. Guinea is an extensive
district on the west of Africa. It is north-west of Angola.

l. 22. **moral,** opposed to physical, as on p. 22, l. 23.

l. 27. **just as reasonable,** that is, just as unreasonable. The
lover in the play, who was at a distance from his beloved, wished
that it might be possible for them to come together in a moment
of time. So English politicians complained of the distance which
separated America from England, and made the task of governing
it more difficult. The two lines quoted by Burke are given in
Martinus Scriblerus, ch. xi., where this "modest request of two
absent lovers" is given as an example of the Hyperbole, or
Impossible. See Elwin and Courthope's edition of Pope, vol. x.,
p. 381. "The memoirs of Scriblerus extend only to the first
book of a work, projected in concert by Pope, Swift, and
Arbuthnot, who used to meet in the time of Queen Anne, and
denominated themselves *the Scriblerus Club.* Their purpose was
to censure the abuses of learning by a fictitious life of an infatu-
ated scholar. They were dispersed; the design was never completed; and Warburton laments its miscarriage, as an event
very disastrous to polite letters" (*Johnson's Life of Pope*).

l. 30. **alterative,** which can change the Americans.

l. 31. **not quite easy,** absolutely impossible. In saying that 'there are difficulties in the way of removing the Atlantic,' Burke is laughing at those who thought that America could be governed as if the Atlantic did not exist.

l. 33. **that,** connected with *if*, on which the sentence depends. "If it is desperate, and if it seems certain that the spirit will continue."

P. 31, l. 2. **a great deal too big,** You cannot take legal proceedings against a whole nation, or put a whole people in the dock.

l. 3. **should,** we should say *would*.

l. 4. **in reason and policy,** common sense tells us that there is a difference between a local riot and a general rebellion, and it is unwise to make no difference between them.

l. 10. **pedantic,** *Pedantry* means the unreasonable ostentation, or the affectation, of knowledge supposed to characterise a teacher (pedant). In a wider sense it denotes an absurd respect for mere form, and a preference of the letter to the spirit. It may of course be argued that a general rebellion is an offence, and that offences are punishable by law. The answer to this must be that there are different kinds of offences.

l. 12. **drawing up an indictment,** framing a charge.

l. 14. **Sir Edward Coke,** When Raleigh was prosecuted for complicity in plots against James I., Sir Edward Coke, then Attorney General, conducted the prosecution. He disgraced himself by the abusive epithets which he addressed to Raleigh, calling him 'a monster,' 'a viper,' 'the rankest traitor in all England,' 'a damnable atheist,' and 'a spider of hell.' Coke afterwards rose to be Chief Justice of the King's Bench and Privy Councillor. From the time that he was first raised to the Bench in 1606 he became one of the greatest champions of law as against arbitrary government. He is one of the greatest of English writers on law.

l. 15. **at the bar,** the part of the court where the prisoner stands.

l. 16. **ripe,** ready, prepared : **gravest public bodies,** the Colonial Assemblies.

l. 18. **charged with,** entrusted with the care of.

l. 19. **upon the very same title,** viz., as a popular representative. *Title* means a legal right.

l. 20. **for sober men,** etc., not becoming for moderate men. **It is a most extravagant proposal.**

l. 22. **Perhaps, Sir,** etc. Notice once more how Burke sees in particular events and proposals an occasion for general reflections and an enunciation of general principles. The proposal to punish America involves the assumption that every assertion of a right or every request for a privilege on the part of a subject country is criminal. This suggests to Burke a consideration of the nature and limits of imperial authority. In his speech on American taxation he had argued that the function of the central government is to supervise, not to supersede, local authorities.

l. 27. **and nothing but,** etc., when all the subjects are slaves there will of course be no assertion of independence. But universal slavery is like universal death. In a slave population all feeling and energy are dead. Who would wish to purchase uniform submission at the cost of universal slavery ?

l. 32. **ill blood,** bad feeling.

l. 35. **The claim of a privilege,** etc., in the very act of asking any one for a favour we allow that it rests with him to grant or to refuse it. The Latin word *privilegium* meant a law against, or an ordinance in favour of, an individual.

P. 32, l. 8. **to beat,** because the drum gives the signal.

l. 9. **under the ban,** to proclaim them rebels. The word *ban* (Low Latin, *bannum*, a proclamation) always signifies that it is a punishment which is proclaimed. For instance, it is applied to an interdict, or Papal sentence of excommunication.

l. 10. **no distinction,** viz., between different kinds of obedience. They will argue that submission is in itself slavery.

l. 14. **not .. quite convenient,** notice how the effect is heightened by the ironical understatement.

l. 20. **frightens me,** I am afraid of deciding unjustly in my own favour.

l. 23. **judicial,** impartial.

l. 26. **as often decided,** Cf. "In all disputes between the people and their rulers the presumption is at least upon a par in favour of the people. Experience may perhaps justify me in going further. When popular discontents have been very prevalent, it may well be affirmed and supported that there has been generally something found amiss in the constitution or in the conduct of government " (*Present Discontents*).

l. 28. **abstract,** considered without reference to the fairness or expediency of exercising it in any given circumstances.

l. 31. **the most odious,** etc. In his speech on American taxation Burke talked of 'the odious and suspicious *summum ius*,'

E

i.e. rigour of the law. There is a saying, *summum ius summa iniuria* : the utmost rigour of the law is the extreme of injustice. Equity, or a regard to the spirit of the law, must temper the administration of it.

l. 34. **the same party,** viz., the Americans.

l. 35. **a civil litigant,** a party to a suit in which a right is the subject of dispute ; in this case, England's right to tax : **a culprit,** etc., because, if I decide that England has the right, it will follow that the Americans have been guilty in denying and resisting the right.

P. 33, l. 1. **whose moral quality,** their guilt or innocence.

l. 2. **Men are every now,** etc. A man may occasionally find himself in the unusual position of having to decide in a cause affecting his own interests ; but, because the decision rests with him, he is not free to decide as he pleases.

l. 5. **There is, Sir, also,** etc. If it is expedient to try Americans as traitors, why have not those, who have pronounced them traitors, brought them to trial ?

l. 10. **addressed,** presented an address to the Sovereign, asking for the application of this statute. By the statute of Henry VIII. persons accused of treasonable acts outside England could be brought to trial in England. The statute was directed against those whose offences were committed where England had no jurisdiction, and Burke more than once urged the iniquity of applying it to the Americans. The excuse offered for it was that no jury in America would convict an American.

l. 16. **modes of public coercion,** the closing of Boston harbour and the stoppage of the trade of the colonies with England were really a blockade, which is an attempt to reduce a hostile power by starvation.

l. 17. **qualified,** short of an absolute declaration of war.

l. 20. **these juridical ideas,** the plan of bringing the Americans to trial for treason.

l. 25. **for the time,** considering how short the time is over which they have extended.

l. 35. **of criminal process,** of bringing them to trial as rebels.

P. 34, l. 2. **if you please,** if you prefer the expression. Burke has already said that they would have preferred a more accommodating spirit in the Americans (p. 23, l. 28).

l. 8. **seal,** from the Latin *sigillum,* a diminutive of *signum,* a sign, or mark.

l. 19. **startle,** start, show signs of astonishment. We now use the word transitively.

l. 24. **the policy,** what it is expedient to do.

l. 26. **a power excepted,** this was Chatham's contention.

l. 28. **polity,** the Greek word for constitution, or form of government.

l. 29. **the charter of nature,** See note on p. 20, l. 8.

l. 36. **there is no sure footing,** etc., it is not possible to decide with certainty between them.

P. 35, l. 1. **the great Serbonian bog,** (Milton, *P. L.* ii. 592). The Serbonian bog is the Lake Serbonis. Damietta is a town near the easternmost mouth of the Nile, and Mount Casius is on the coast, further east.

l. 3. **I do not intend,** I shall not, as many men deserving of respect have done, engage myself in the discussion of that insoluble question. No reader can fail to be struck by the sentences which follow.

l. 13. **your evidence-room,** the room in which a man keeps his securities, and all legal documents proving his right to his property. A **title** means a legal right. England's *titles* are of course preserved in acts of parliament, charters, etc.

l. 14. **magazines,** storehouses, but used especially with reference to military stores.

l. 17. **my suit,** what I am anxious to gain or keep, viz., America. Burke has already said that the value of the object would be diminished by a contest (p. 16, l. 32). Here he means that they might be beaten in the contest, and so lose America altogether.

l. 21. **by a unity of spirit,** etc., our motive or policy should be the same, whatever subordinate country we are dealing with, viz., to make all contented. The mode of producing contentment will differ from country to country, and will vary with times and circumstances. Burke's language is a reminiscence of a passage in St. Paul's 1*st Ep. to the Corinthians,* xii. 4, " Now there are diversities of gifts, but the same Spirit. And there are differences of administrations, but the same Lord. And there are diversities of operations, but it is the same God which worketh all in all."

l. 36. **to admit ... into an interest,** etc., to allow them to share the benefits of it.

P. 36, l. 6. **upon its understood principle,** as an act the avowed object of which was revenue, and not control of trade. A mere repeal of duties is not now sufficient, because the Americans will not feel sure that it will not be followed by an imposition of other duties, just as the repeal of the Stamp Act was followed by Townshend's Act, and all the acts of coercion which have been passed to enforce it. To give the Americans confidence, and to protect yourselves against temptation in future, you must give and record a formal promise that the policy of taxing for revenue has been once and for all abandoned.

l. 8. **an unconditional abatement**, an absolute and unqualified abandonment. To *abate* means, literally, to *beat down*.

l. 15. **I have taken ... measure**, I am mistaken as to what it is. An equivalent expression is, "I have not gauged it correctly."

l. 17. **American financiers**, men who form their opinions as to what should be done on a consideration of what we shall gain or lose in money. Burke's policy was not opposed on the ground that the repeal of the taxes would diminish the English revenue, and would throw upon the English charges which the Americans ought to bear. It was opposed through fear that repeal might lead to a demand for further concessions.

l. 18. **too acute**, too sharp, too clever. We see danger where there is none : **too exquisite**, too careful or ingenious. A wise man, when he is in danger, thinks first how he is to get out of it. A drowning man would not refuse help for fear that, when he got to land, his helper might ask for a reward. The word *exquisite* means, literally, *sought out*. The ordinary meaning of the word is *excellent*, because that which is excellent can only be found by careful search.

l. 28. **a gentleman**, a Mr. Rice.

l. 32. **the arguments**, viz., that the commercial regulations are neither oppressive to America nor profitable to England.

P. 37, l. 1. **the noble lord**, etc. See on p. 6, l. 35 : **shall**, we should say *will*. The word *shall* connotes obligation or compulsion ; so it was not unfrequently used to emphasize the conviction that what was predicted was quite certain to happen.

l. 5. **by the natural**, etc. They trade with us because they find it profitable to do so.

l. 7. **in this posture of the debate**, when it is necessary to reply to the argument that it is unfair to add the burden of taxation to the burden of the trade laws, and to enrich ourselves by taxation as well as by commercial monopoly.

l. 10. **experience**, our having tried and failed : **the nature of things**, the character of the Americans and their distance from England.

l. 13. **press themselves**, they are so obvious that none can help seeing them.

l. 16. **trance**, a temporary suspension of animation.

l. 17. **as a counter-guard**, etc., for fear that, if we repeal the taxes, we shall have to repeal the trade laws too

l. 21. **members,** parts ; literally, limbs.

l. 24. **the pamphlet,** written by Dr. Tucker. See note on p. 26, l. 24.

l. 26. **idolizing,** To idolize means to worship. An idol is an image worshipped as a god.

l. 27. **still ... in former times,** Now that our trade is so wide and so firmly established, the trade of any one country is less important to us than it was in earlier times. A firm that does a large business is indifferent to the loss of an individual customer. To a small trader every customer is of importance.

l. 29. **the market,** literally, the place where they can sell their goods ; and so, the sale of them. If they might sell where they liked, they could sell much more than they do at present.

P. 38, l. 6. **we have to see,** etc. There are two very simple tests to decide what the real grievance of the Americans is—first, see what they complained of first ; second, remove the taxes, and see if their complaints cease.

l. 16. **with decency,** It is unseemly to charge them with lying when you cannot support the charge.

l. 19. **not on their own acts,** etc., not for something which they have really done, but for something which you suppose they are going to do.

l. 22. **converting your ill-will,** etc. They are to be punished on account of your ill-natured suspicions.

l. 23. **But,** The word introduces the objection of an imaginary opponent.

l. 24. **fact,** because previous concessions have not been followed by further demands : **reason,** because the natural tendency of kindness is to beget contentment and goodwill.

l. 25. **panic,** unreasonable, ungrounded. The sudden fright which sometimes seizes bodies of men was thought by the Greeks to be inspired by the god Pan.

l. 29. **to make a rule for itself?** to make it an exception to the general rule that a sovereign may properly remove grievances. Burke emphasizes the reasonableness of his own arguments by showing the absurdity of their opposites.

l. 35. **divinations,** guesses.

P. 39, l. 6. **I set out,** etc. Instead of inventing a plan of my own, I determined upon proposing to do what our ancestors had already done in similar cases.

l. 17. **consult the genius of,** etc., do what they thought he would have done. Philip II., son of the Emperor Charles V. and Isabella of Portugal, ascended the throne of Spain in 1556. This dynasty continued until the year 1700. Charles V. inherited the throne of Spain from his mother.

l. 19. **the most perfect standard,** he was a stupid man and a most intolerant bigot. He married Queen Mary of England.

l. 21. **consult the genius of,** etc., follow constitutional precedents.

l. 23. **it was ... piety,** that is, in the attitude of mind proper to one who listens for the inspired utterances of Deity. See on p. 18, l. 33.

l. 24. **capital,** leading, chief.

l. 27. **by a despotic power,** it was split up into a number of independent chieftainships. The basis of social organization among the Irish Celts was *the sept,* corresponding to the Scotch clan. The country was conquered by Henry II. in 1172.

l. 29. **is disputed,** it certainly did not exist according to the present form. Even the Saxon Witangemote, or assembly of wise men, sank very early into a gathering of temporal and spiritual peers and royal officials. The Great Council of the Norman kings was not any more representative than the Witangemote had been. It was a royal court of feudal vassals. It had no power of refusing grants demanded by the crown, and it was only summoned at the pleasure of the crown. From the time of Henry II., however, its meetings became more regular, and its functions more important. The great reforms which marked his reign were carried in the Great Council, and even financial matters were suffered to be debated there (Green, *Short History of the English People,* pp. 167-8).

l. 32. **she instantly communicated,** the Irish Parliament was always subordinate to that of England. The famous *Poynings' Act,* passed in 1494, subjected Ireland to all laws passed by the English Parliament, and deprived the Irish Parliament of all power of initiating legislation. No measures could be submitted to it which had not previously received the sanction of the King and the English Privy Council.

l. 36. **the roots,** etc., our representative system has grown out of the occasional assemblies of feudal vassals summoned by the Norman kings. In process of time the crown found it necessary to summon certain lesser barons and knights from each shire, because grants made in the Council were only binding on those members who attended it. Theoretically, the knights represented only the lesser barons, but as from the 13th century they were, in practice, elected by the whole body of rural freeholders in the shire from which they were sent, they became *representatives of the shire* (Green). The word **feudal** is from feud, a fief, that is, land held from a superior. Fief is from a German word *vieh,* signifying cattle, and thence property.

P. 40, l. 3. **of weight and consequence,** Not only did the Great Charter regulate the form of the Great Council, but it first recognized the powers of the Council over taxation, and established the principle that no burden beyond the customary feudal aids might be imposed "save by the Common Council of the realm" (Read Green, pp. 167-171).

l. 4. **churlishly,** boorishly. The word churl, applied to the Saxon serf, naturally came to signify a rude fellow.

l. 7. **to all Ireland,** it was restricted to the district occupied by the English settlers, which was called "the English Pale."

l. 9. **Your standard,** your power, literally, your national flag.

l. 11. **Sir John Davis,** Chief-Justice under James I. He published a book called *Discovery of the true causes why Ireland was never entirely subdued till his Majesty's happy reign.*

l. 13. **was five hundred years,** referring to the pacification of the island in the time of King James. In the following sentences he refers to the attempt made by the Earl of Essex, under Elizabeth, to put down the rebellions which were caused mainly by the attempt to force the Catholic religion on the people. At the death of Elizabeth the flight of the native leaders left the island at the mercy of James. But the island was not subdued. This was not effected until the terrible conquest of William III., when "the conquered people, in Swift's bitter words of contempt, beame 'hewers of wood and drawers of water' to their conquerors. From that time until the very eve of the French Revolution Ireland ceased to be a source of terror and anxiety to England" (Green).

l. 16. **civility,** civilization.

l. 18. **It was not,** etc., it was not conquered by force, but won over by the benefits of English rule.

l. 19. **From that time,** that is, from the time of the settlement of James I. By a *general* parliament he means one in which Irishmen as well as Englishmen in Ireland could sit.

l. 21. **You changed,** etc., alluding to the occupation of great part of the country by English settlers, and to the establishment of the Protestant religion.

l. 23. **kings,** viz., the English sovereigns.

l. 26. **by usurpation,** viz., by Cromwell.

l. 27. **the restoration,** viz., of Charles II.

l. 28. **Revolution,** that, namely, of 1688. It was *glorious* to Burke, because it was an assertion of Whig principles, which he regarded as constitutional principles. It prevented the attempted perversion by the Stuarts of the English government into a despotism. Burke called it 'a revolution not made but prevented.'

l. 31. **our strength and ornament,** unfortunately Ireland was rather a source of weakness and a discredit to England. The political disabilities of the Catholic inhabitants, and the superior privileges of the resident English Protestants were of themselves sufficient to make Ireland disaffected.

l. 34. **on the hinge of,** when they were impending. He refers to the treatment which the country experienced from Cromwell and William III.

l. 36. **they make an exception,** The common saying that 'the exception proves the rule' is, literally, a contradiction in terms. A rule is a statement of what always happens. If a thing happens always, there are no exceptions to it. If there are exceptions to it, it does not happen always. What the saying means is that our belief in a rule is strengthened if we can see why an apparent exception to it is not a real exception. We must not argue to what the normal policy of a country is from its policy in the exceptional circumstances of a revolution.

P. **41,** l. 1. **None of your own,** etc. If England is to have no privileges which have not at some time and under some circumstances been suspended, she will have none at all.

l. 4. **lucrative,** ironical. If you had been in the habit of taking money instead of receiving it, you would not have got so much as you have got. *Supply* is a technical word for revenue. The House of Commons, when considering the Budget, sits "in Committee of *Supply*."

l. 6. **Your Irish pensioners,** all recipients of pensions who are paid out of Irish revenues.

l. 10. **that only source,** viz., free grants as opposed to exactions of money.

l. 14. **by Edward the First,** Llewellyn, Prince of Wales, was killed in a skirmish in 1282, and with his death the independence of Wales expired (Green, p. 162).

l. 18. **lords marchers,** literally, lords of the boundaries.

l. 20. **heterogeneous,** comprising elements differing in kind. It differed from an ordinary military occupation in being permanent. It differed from ordinary government in that it preserved order by military terrorism.

l. 23. **all civil power,** etc., this power is delegated to him. During the occupation of a country by a hostile force, necessity may justify the commander-in-chief in dealing with the civil population according to military law.

l. 24. **the genius,** the character, or spirit.

l. 25. **restive,** see on p. 17, l. 28.

l. 26. **composed,** quieted for a time.

l. 30. **incursion**, inroads, raids.

l. 35. **with something more**, etc., you have done by executive order what perhaps required an Act of Parliament.

P. 42, l. 2. **an instruction**, an order to General Gage, the English commander in America.

l. 4. **as you have done**, viz., by reviving the statute of Henry VIII. : **with more hardship**, because America is farther off. As Burke points out in his *Letter to the Sheriffs of Bristol*, an American, if put on his trial in England, could not call witnesses in his favour.

l. 8. **fairs**, from the Latin *feriæ*, literally, a holiday. A *fair* combines business with amusement. When communications were less perfect than they are now, it was the custom to hold periodical markets in each district, which were called *fairs*.

l. 9. **from fisheries**, etc., referring to the Act of Lord North.

l. 13. **we rub our hands**, a sign of being pleased. Burke's opponents will argue that the coercion of Wales is a precedent for the coercion of America. Burke replies that the ill success of the policy in Wales should be a warning not to try the same policy in America.

l. 16. **rid**, rode, oppressed : **an incubus**, a nightmare.

l. 20. **The march**, etc., men are slow to learn.

l. 22. **vexation to violence**, "His mischief shall return upon his own head, and his violent dealings shall come down upon his own pate" (*Psalm*, vii. 16).

l. 24. **the ill husbandry**, the unthriftiness. You will get no money from those whom you oppress. You will not enrich yourselves by attempting to plunder your subjects. *Husbandry*, like *economy*, means, literally, the management of a house.

l. 25. **the tyranny**, etc., cf. p. 29, l. 10, 'An Englishman is the unfittest person,' etc.

l. 30. **the entire and perfect rights**, etc. Burke means that it corresponded entirely to the Declaratory Act passed by Rockingham's government.

l. 33. **the marches**, P. 41, l. 18. A *march*, in the sense of a boundary, is the same word as *mark*.

P. 43, l. 4. **as by a charm**, as if by a spell : as if by magic.

l. 7. **When the day-star**, etc. When they were cheered by the light of British freedom. "We have also a more sure word of prophecy ; whereunto ye do well that ye take heed, as unto a light that shineth in a dark place, until the day dawn, *and the day star arise in your hearts*" (2 *Peter*, i. 19).

l. 9. **Simul alba**, etc., political disturbances subsided, as a storm at sea subsides when the constellation of Castor and

Pollux, or the Twins, rises. The quotation is from the Latin poet, Horace, *Od.* i. 12. 27.

l. 21. **the county palatine**, this name was given to the district subject to the jurisdiction of a Frankish *count*. In England these counties were governed by a temporal or spiritual peer. The word *palatine* is from the Latin *palatium*, a palace. Chester and Durham were no doubt made separate regalities on account of their proximity to the frontiers of Wales and Scotland. Chester and Durham became palatine under William I. Chester had not merely its own courts, judges, constable, and steward, but a parliament, and was not represented in the national Parliament till 1549. Cheshire was assimilated by Henry VIII. Durham ceased to be a county palatine under its bishop in 1836 (Chambers).

l. 30. **in most humble wise**, the order of the words is, ' The inhabitants shew in most humble wise (fashion) unto,' etc. *Shown* is the 3rd person plural of show. *Wise,* in the sense of manner, occurs in like-wise, otherwise. Another form of *wise* is *guise.*

l. 32. **where**, whereas.

P. 44, l. 1. **to have**, from having : **knights and burgesses** correspond to our county and borough members. For *knights* see p. 39, l. 36. A *burgess* means, literally, one belonging to a borough.

l. 3. **disherisons**, used in the general sense of *deprivations.*

l. 10. **as far forth as**, to the same extent as.

l. 13. **ne**, nor.

l. 21. **audacious**, this is the epithet which would be applied to it by those who were zealous for the absolute powers of Parliament.

l. 22. **a libel**, a seditious publication.

l. 24. **toss it over the table**, refuse to receive it. In his speech on American taxation Burke says of remonstrances from two American colonies that " they were suppressed : they were put under the table " : **Did they burn it**, etc., an extreme mode of marking its criminality.

l. 26. **without softening**, etc., without in any way toning it down.

l. 29. **and consecrated**, etc. By adopting it as a preamble to an Act of Parliament they made any violation of its principle equivalent to an act of sacrilege.

l. 35. **superstition,** an irrational worship of what does not deserve worship. The proper remedy for superstition is a true religion, not no religion.

P. 45, l. 2. **the pale,** the limits. The word signifies literally *a stake*, and so a place fenced in.

l. 5. **without affecting ... equity,** just as Burke wished now to make a concession to the Americans as a matter of fairness, leaving the question of right untouched.

l. 26. **But,** the word introduces the objection of an imaginary opponent. **What,** marks a contemptuous rejection of such an argument.

l. 27. **electric,** magnetic. It might with some plausibility be argued that the Welsh were as good as represented, because the English members knew their wants and would look after their interests. But this could not be said of a distant country like America, of which Englishmen knew nothing.

P. 46, l. 5. **Opposuit natura,** Juvenal, *Sat.* x. 152, says that Hannibal in his march towards Italy overcame the snowy Alps with which *nature barred his way.* Burke, of course, is referring to the ocean which separated England and America.

l. 9. **see my way to it,** a common expression for, I do not see how it is to be managed.

l. 11. **the arm,** etc.. we are not unable to remove their griev- ances, simply because we cannot give them representation in our own Parliament. "The Lord's hand is not shortened, that it cannot save" (*Isaiah,* lix. 1).

l. 19. **unproductive invention,** limited or barren ingenuity : **to tax,** to call upon it to suggest a plan. When Parliament in committee of supply has sanctioned the revenue to be raised in the year, it goes into committee of *ways and means* to consider by what taxation the revenue is to be raised.

l. 21. **the Republic,** an ideal commonwealth sketched by Plato, the Greek philosopher. The *Utopia* of Sir Thomas More was first published in 1516. It was really a criticism of English laws and customs, just as the *Republic* of Plato was a satire on Greek politics. The word Utopia has come to mean any impracticable ideal. The *Oceana* in which Harrington set forth his ideal of a commonwealth was published in 1656. Oceana is England.

l. 23. **It is before me,** etc., it is obvious : **the rude swain, etc.,** "and the dull swain Treads on it daily with his clouted shoon" (Milton, *Comus,* 633). *Clouted shoon* means *patched shoes.*

l. 25. **for the theory,** as regards the principle.

l. 33. **by grant,** by voluntary contributions from the American Assemblies.

l. 34. **the legal competency,** this had been disputed.

P. 47, l. 1. **dutiful.** loyal.

l. 3. **supply,** see on p. 41, l. 4.

l. 8. **I think,** etc., I think that the adoption of my measure will secure peace to the British Empire. The metaphor is suggested by the temple which the Romans dedicated to Concord.

l. 12. **with but tolerable,** etc., if you only avoid gross mistakes.

l. 17. **management,** skill.

l. 28. **the description,** the persons named in it.

l. 30. **The second is like unto,** etc., a reminiscence of *Matt.* xxii. 37, "Jesus said unto him, Thou shalt love the Lord thy God with all thy heart, and with all thy soul, and with all thy mind. This is the first and great commandment. *And the second is like unto it,* Thou shalt love thy neighbour as thyself."

l. 36. **by lack whereof,** for want of which representation.

P. 48, l. 2. **commonwealth,** general well-being. *Wealth* is the same as *weal,* prosperity.

l. 10. **Non meus,** etc., Horace, *Sat.* ii. 2. 1 ; imitated by Pope, *Sat.* ii. 2—

"Hear Bethel's sermon, one not versed in schools,
But strong in sense, and wise without the rules."

l. 18. **It would be,** etc., it would be an act of sacrilege to tamper with that which is to produce peace.

l. 20. **I would not violate,** etc., he still keeps up the metaphor of a mason building an altar to Peace. The Latin word *ingenuus* is used in the sense of 'native to the country.' Lucretius applied it in this sense to springs of water, and Juvenal to stone. In plain English Burke's meaning is—"I shrank from translating into the polished phraseology of modern times the rough but venerable diction of these ancient statutes."

l. 23. **tampering,** meddling. We generally speak of 'tampering with' something : **restless,** who cannot be satisfied with what they find ; always anxious for change.

l. 24. **I can neither wander,** etc., I cannot be at a loss or make a mistake.

l. 26. **not to be wise,** etc., a possible rendering of a phrase which occurs in Paul's 1*st Epistle to the Corinthians,* iv. 6. In the English Bible it is rendered, "that ye might learn in us *not to think of men above that which is written,* that no one of you be puffed up for one against another." Bisping's *Catholic Commentary* gives as a possible rendering—"that you may learn from us not to think (of yourselves or your position) beyond what is written" : and he says that by 'what is written' may be meant either Christ's exhortation to humility, or Scripture in general, which often exhorts men not to extol themselves, or particular passages of Scripture, such as "The wisdom of this world is foolishness with God. For it is written, He taketh the

wise in their own craftiness.   And again, The Lord knoweth the
thoughts of the wise, that they are vain" (1 *Cor.* iii. 19, 20).

l. 27. **to use nothing else,** etc.   Paul, in his *2nd Epistle to
Timothy,* i. 13, says, "Hold fast *the form of sound words* which
thou hast heard of me, in faith and love which is in Christ Jesus."
Burke means that it is as dangerous to deviate from the exact
words of Parliament as it is to tamper with the actual text of
divine revelation.

l. 34. **those who are resolved,** etc., those who are determined
always to find some weak point in what is said by others.

P. 49, l. 17. **of George II.,**   The Act of George II. imposed a
duty on sugar, molasses, and rum imported by the Americans
from the French colonies in the West Indies.

l. 23. **Lord Hillsborough,** Secretary of State for the Colonies.

l. 28. **the noble lord,** p. 6, l. 35.

P. 50, l. 1. **on the paper,** in the resolution which I am sub-
mitting to you.

l. 7. **freemen,** the technical word to describe those who have
inherited the full rights of citizens :   **freeholders,** freehold is the
name of a form of land tenure.   Estates held for life and estates
of inheritance rank as freehold.   "The freeholders of a county
were constitutent members of the ancient county court ; they had
formerly the right to vote in the election of county coroners :
and freehold property of the value required by modern statutes
is a qualification for jurymen and parliamentary electors, and for
certain public offices" (*Chambers' Encyclopædia,* s.v. *freehold*).

l. 10. **the several usage,** the practice that prevails in each of
them.

l. 16. **the public offices,** those, namely, of the English Government.

l. 17. **paradoxically,** a paradox means, literally, whatever runs
counter to commonly received opinion.   Burke is thinking of
Grenville who held that the Colonies could not legally grant any
revenue to the Crown.

l. 22. **the law servants,** such as the Attorney-General and
Solicitor-General.

l. 23. **if the crown could be responsible,** whatever is nominally
done by the Sovereign is done by the Ministry who are his
responsible advisers.

l. 27. **impeachable offences,** impeachment is the technical name
for a charge of unconstitutional action against a Minister of the
crown.   Burke regarded impeachment as the great safeguard of
the English constitution.

l. 32. **their own unfounded theories**, viz., that the colonial assemblies cannot make grants to the crown.

P. 51, l. 6. **the Indian wars**, the frequent wars with the North American Indians on their frontiers.

l. 7. **so high**, so far back. They were engaged in wars with France and Spain from 1690-7. In 1710 their struggle was with France.

l. 10. **the journals**, the records of proceedings in Parliament. Contributions made ' on requisition ' and voluntary contributions did not, of course, appear in the journals.

l. 13. **1748**, the year of the peace of Aix-la-Chapelle. Cape Breton, which was colonized by the French, was then restored to France.

l. 23. **advanced**, namely to England. They were obliged to borrow in order to give England what she wanted.

l. 26. **to us**, to the House of Commons.

l. 33. **1756**, the first year of the Seven Years' War.

P. 52, l. 15. **had gone beyond their abilities**, had granted us more than they could afford.

l. 26. **honourable to them and to you**, as showing their loyalty and your gratitude.

l. 27. **mortal**, fatal : **miserable**, contemptible.

l. 28. **the misguided people**, the English.

l. 29. **an unhappy system**, viz., that of taxing America. With all this evidence of the liberality of the Americans, it can never again be asserted that they must be taxed because they will not contribute.

P. 53, l. 4. **state**, statement : **those untaxed people**, those who were represented as paying no taxes were burdened with the repayment of a debt which they had incurred on behalf of England.

l. 7. **sinking**, extinguishing. It is a technical term for paying off. A sum accumulated for the payment of debt is called ' a Sinking Fund.'

l. 9. **sanguine**, hopeful.

l. 13. **requisitions**, Used in its technical sense of demands addressed by the English Secretary of State to the colonies for grants.

l. 14. **our tone became too high**, We became too imperious; we thought it beneath us to ask, and we resolved to take.

l. 17. **the sense**, what they felt and thought : **the crown**, referring to the message from the King quoted on p. 51.

l. 24. **let them and that,** etc.   I will say no more about it.

l. 27. **the melancholy burthen,** etc., unhappily it fills and dis-figures every page.   The word *burden* means the refrain of a song.   It is the French word *bourdon,* which means a drone-bee, and was probably intended to express its meaning by its sound.

P. 54, l. 2. **the utmost rights,** etc., viz., taxation of the un-represented.   He uses the word *utmost* because it was doubtful whether this was a 'right of legislature' at all.

l. 13. **imagination... fact ... enjoyment ... hope,** Will you throw away a certain revenue from voluntary grants on the chance of getting one by taxation?   A bird in the hand is worth two in the bush.

l. 18. **to be moved,** to be formally proposed to the House ; to be voted on.

l. 22. **plantations,** The word was used where we should use colonies or settlements.   It no longer bears this sense.   The Latin word *planta* means a shoot : and a colony is an offshoot of the mother country.

l. 23. **drawbacks,** a drawback is a total or partial refund of a duty, paid either upon imported goods or upon home productions subject to excise, when they were exported.   The object was to encourage exportation.   Commercial regulations at that time were made not so much with a view to the interests of trade as with a view to the accumulation of money for the maintenance of the country's military supremacy.   The exporter was encour-aged because to export is to sell to foreigners, that is, to bring money into the country.

l. 28. **clandestine running,** smuggling.

P. 55, l. 3. **in the execution of the law,** Massachusetts being regarded as in a state of rebellion, it was thought that justice would not be done there to any who might be accused of com-mitting acts of violence while upholding the law.   Such persons, therefore, were to be removed for trial either to another colony or to England.

l. 8. **the better regulating,** See Introduction.

l. 16. **during the king's pleasure,** that is, until the Govern-ment thinks proper to restore the rights.

l. 21. **the restraining bill,** the bill which is alluded to in the opening paragraph of this speech.

l. 26. **partially,** unfairly, not impartially.

l. 30. **though the crown,** etc.   See on p. 19, l. 18.

P. 56, l. 5. **the sheriff,** the officer whose business it is to see that the judgments of the court are executed.   It is corrupted from shire-reeve, an officer of the shire.

l. 6. **returning officer,** the officer who summoned the jury. This duty was by the Act transferred to the sheriff. The object, of course, was to obtain a jury unfavourable to any one charged with an offence by Government.

l. 9. **The act,** etc. See on p. 55, l. 3.

l. 19. **the greatest treasons,** etc. For instance, Englishmen may organize a conspiracy against their own sovereign abroad. In the year 1858 an attempt was made on the life of Napoleon III. in Paris, and the French complained bitterly that the conspirators had been allowed to arrange their plans and manufacture their weapons in England.

l. 26. **a settled salary to the offices,** in the colonies in New England where the salaries were very low and were only voted from year to year, there were great complaints of the partiality of the judges.

P. 57, l. 2. **the courts of admiralty,** so called as having jurisdiction in the case of offences committed on the sea.

l. 6. **the more decent maintenance,** at that time they received a part of the fines which they inflicted.

l. 10. **the Act of Navigation,** The original object of this Act, as passed by Cromwell in 1651, was to transfer the profits of the carrying trade from Holland to England. In Burke's day it was an accepted principle that the mother country might regulate the trade of her colonies for her own benefit. The trade of the colonies was confined to ships built in England or America, and manned by crews of whom two-thirds were British sailors. There were certain 'enumerated' articles which they might sell to England only. If they wanted to import many foreign products, they were obliged to do it through England. They were forbidden to export, and, in some cases, even to produce commodities in which they could have undersold England. They were forced to buy certain commodities which were of great importance to them, sugar, molasses and rum, from English colonies, though they could have bought them cheaper from French or Spanish colonies.

l. 16. **The congress,** that which met at Philadelphia. See Introduction.

l. 18. **consequential,** those 'corollary to' (p. 47, l. 5) his six fundamental propositions.

l. 22. **congruity,** consistency. Those who accept the six cannot logically refuse the three; but Burke hopes that even the rejection of the three will not prevent the establishment of permanent peace between England and America.

l. 31. **I prove too much,** namely, that if we have no right to tax the Americans, we have no right to legislate for them.

P. 58, l. 1. **wishing as little**, etc., as he had shown by his support of the Declaratory Act.

l. 6. **Mr. Grenville,** He had quoted the Act to show that there had been taxation without representation.

l. 10. **Lord Chatham,** In his reply to Grenville, Chatham said, "I come not here armed at all points with law cases and Acts of Parliament, with the statute-book doubled down in dogs'-ears, to defend the cause of liberty. If I had, I myself would have cited the two cases of Chester and Durham. I would have cited them to show that even under arbitrary reigns Parliament was ashamed of taxing a people without their consent, and allowed them representation " (Stanhope, v. p. 134).

l. 11. **no less,** he supported the privileges of the Americans as strongly as Grenville did the rights of Parliament.

l. 19. **to the case of subsidies,** and not of legislation.

l. 20. **falls in exactly with,** agrees with, resembles. Here again Burke argues that the question of taxing those who are unrepresented is, and has been acknowledged by Parliament to be, one which is to be regarded from the point of view, not of right, but of fairness.

l. 28. **in any cool hour,** when not under the excitement of anger.

l. 36. **illation,** inference.

P. 59, l. 1. **any given part,** the Crown and the two Houses of Parliament are the three parts of the British constitution, which is thus an organic balance of monarchical, democratical, and aristocratic elements. When defending the House of Commons the Englishman argues on democratic principles, but he does not push them to the extreme, because he knows that the democratic element in his constitution is combined with, and must, therefore, be limited by its other elements. Burke develops this point at some length in his *Appeal to the Old Whigs.*

l. 2. **or even the whole of it together,** an Englishman may submit to many limitations of his freedom which it would be hard to reconcile with his views of the English constitution. But he does not kick against them. Provided that he gets the maximum of advantage with the minimum of restraint, he is content.

l. 5. **All government,** in this life we are not to expect absolute perfection or perfect happiness, but must be content with the highest degree of either that is attainable under the circumstances. A compromise is an agreement arrived at by each party surrendering something. We must not expect to get all that we could desire, but must be prepared to give and take. Cf. "The rights of men in governments are their advantages : and these are often in balances between differences of good ; in compromises sometimes between good and evil, and sometimes between evil and evil": and "one advantage is (by the English) as little as possible sacrificed to another. We compensate, we reconcile, we balance" (*Reflections on the Revolution in France*).

l. 7. **We balance inconveniences,** we weigh one against the other and choose the least. As there must be some inconveniences under any system, this is the only wise course.

l. 9. **we choose rather,** etc. It was a favourite idea with Burke that a tendency to political criticism was a sign of discontent. "The bulk of mankind are not excessively curious concerning any theories, whilst they are really happy : and one sure symptom of an ill-conducted state is the propensity of the people to resort to them" (*Letter to the Sheriffs of Bristol*).

l. 11. **natural,** see on p. 20, l. 8. This is a point on which Burke dwells at great length in his *Reflections on the Revolution in France.* The revolutionists, who contended that governments must respect *the rights of man,* appeared to him to be attempting to reconcile two incompatible things, the freedom of nature with the benefits of society. Burke's argument there is, that an appeal to the rights of men would justify an attack upon all governments. The real rights of men are those advantages which society was instituted to secure, and society cannot subsist without control. If men wish to abandon the state of nature for the state of society, they must submit to those limitations of their natural rights which social life requires. They cannot have the advantages of society and the freedom of nature too. Government is a limitation of man's natural rights for his own good. The extent and the mode of the limitation must depend on circumstances.

l. 13. **communion and fellowship,** the words are from a prayer in the English Church service beginning—"O Almighty God who hast knit together thine elect in one *communion and fellowship,* in the mystical body of thy Son Christ."

l. 15. **the purchase,** the purchase money, the price : **the immediate jewel,** etc., his freedom and self-respect. The phrase is borrowed from Shakespeare's *Othello,* iii. 3. 156—

"Good name in man and woman, dear my lord,
    Is the immediate jewel of their souls."

l. 16. **Though a great house,** etc. The Americans will not purchase the honour of belonging to the English empire at the cost of being England's slaves. Cf. Juvenal, 5. 66, Maxima quaeque domus servis est plena superbis—all the great houses are full of haughty slaves.

l. 20. **None of us,** there is not one of us who, etc.

l. 28. **stake of liberty,** a share of freedom which would be in danger of being lost if any change were attempted. A *stake* means anything hazarded. For instance, it is used to denote the sum which a gambler risks.

l. 30. **the cords of man,** the considerations which influence men. Mr. Payne points out that the phrase is from *Hosea*, xi. 4, "I drew them with *cords of a man*, with bands of love."

l. 32. **metaphysical,** abstract. Burke detested the importation of metaphysical arguments into practical politics. "I do not enter into these metaphysical distinctions : I hate the very sound of them." Men are ruled by considerations of prudence. They act when some advantage is to be gained by acting.

l. 36. **sophistry,** See on p. 12, l. 20. The reference to Aristotle is to *Ethics*, bk. i. ch. 4. Elsewhere Burke says— "The excellence of mathematics and metaphysics is to have but one thing before you ; but he forms the best judgment in all moral disquisitions who has the greatest number and variety of considerations in one view before him, and can take them in with the best possible consideration of the middle results of all."

P. 60, l. 4. **a superintending legislature,** Cf. "I look on the imperial rights of Great Britain, and the privileges which the colonies ought to enjoy under these rights, to be just the most reconcilable things in the world. The Parliament of Great Britain sits at the head of her extensive empire in two capacities : one as the local legislature of this island, providing for all things at home, immediately, and by no other instrument than the executive power.—The other, and I think her nobler capacity, is what I call her *imperial character*, in which, as from the throne of heaven, she superintends all the several inferior legislatures, and guides and controls them all without annihilating any. As all these provincial legislatures are only coordinate to each other, they ought all to be subordinate to her : else they can neither preserve mutual peace, nor hope for mutual justice, nor effectually afford mutual assistance. It is necessary to coerce the negligent, to restrain the violent, and to aid the weak and deficient by the overruling plenitude of her power" (*Speech on American Taxation*).

l. 6. **not the rival,** when it does not attempt to supersede their local legislatures.

l. 13. **to value myself,** to pride myself.

l. 16. **which was preserved entire,** etc. Why should the empire be broken up by the concession to America of the same privilege which was granted, without any evil effects, to Chester and Durham ? A united empire is not one of which every member is absolutely subject to a single power. The suzerainty of England is quite compatible with the existence of local privileges.

l. 23. **not an independent,** See on p. 39, l. 32.

l. 25. **sweetly and harmoniously**, perhaps a reminiscence of Pope, *Essay on Man*, iii. 293—

> "Till jarring int'rests of themselves create
> Th' according music of a well-mixed state."

l. 31. **no other unity**, Burke means that his opponents, who are fomenting discords, are more fairly chargeable with breaking up a united empire.

l. 33. **poor**, humble.

P. 61, l. 11. **a ransom by auction**, See p. 7, l. 3.

l. 16. **It is neither**, etc. It is not taxation because the money is to be offered by them : it is not a grant because the sum is not to be what they choose to give, but what we choose to take.

l. 27. **a state auctioneer**, etc. For the meaning of the expressions in this sentence, see notes on p. 7, ll. 3-7 *seqq*.

l. 32. **the British proportion**, Not only is the share of each colony to be in proportion to its wealth, but the taxation of America as a whole must be to the wealth of America as the taxation of England is to the wealth of England.

l. 34. **by the back-door**, in an irregular manner. Properly all matters relating to money must be introduced, debated, and settled in the House of Commons. Under this proposal the contribution of America would be fixed by the Ministry, and merely submitted for formal sanction to the House.

P. 62, l. 3. **the counsel for**, the agent or representative of. Used in the same sense as when applied to the barrister who appears for a man in court.

l. 6. **ways and means**, See on p. 46, l. 19: **provincial**, because dealing with revenues to be raised in the colonies. The Romans used the word *provinces* to denote their foreign possessions.

l. 7. **it will delight**, it may choose to call itself. Burke speaks contemptuously of it as an innovation.

l. 14. **I really beg pardon**, etc. You must excuse my saying it —it is not a pleasant thing to say—but you know that you are not telling the truth.

l. 17. **their contingent**, their share of the imperial expenditure. Cf. p. 64, l. 2.

l. 18. **the importation**, into America. Such duties would have diminished the sale of English commodities by raising the price of them.

l. 22. **the quantum**, the amount. *Quantum* in Latin means *how much*.

l. 29. **general powers**, powers which they could exercise without specific reference to America.

P. 63, l. 1. **the outcry**, the bidding at the auction.

l. 4. **refuse all composition**, to compound means to obtain exemption from future payments by paying a lump sum down. A debtor is said to compound with his creditors if they, finding that he cannot pay the whole of his debts, agree to accept so much in the pound as a final settlement.

l. 5. **to**, to the amount of. Cf. '*to* your quota,' l. 15.

l. 6. **in principle**, that is, as being imposed by the English Parliament : **as to production**, as to the amount of revenue which they yield.

l. 12. **but at the ports**, that is, you can only levy customs duties.

l. 15. **your quota**, the share which you determine that they ought to pay.

l. 17. **you give its death-wound**, England imposed a tax on English tobacco when it was imported, and she re-exported for sale in foreign countries much of what she imported. By taxing the export in Virginia she would raise the price of it, and so diminish her own import, and, consequently, her foreign sales of it.

l. 19. **the import**, the goods imported by the colony.

l. 26. **are so implicated**, the colonies touch one another at so many points, that a colony, which found its exports or imports taxed, could easily export or import what it wanted through a colony in which no tax was levied, and so evade the taxation. The only way to avoid this would be to levy the same tax in all the colonies. But that would be very unjust, because it would lay the same burden upon those who had, and those who had not, made money contributions.

l. 27. **the bill for prohibiting**, etc. This bill was at first intended to be applied only to the New England colonies, but it was afterwards extended to Pennsylvania, New Jersey, Maryland, Virginia, and South Carolina.

l. 32. **to exonerate**, used in its literal sense of 'to relieve of a burden.' It is now commonly used in the sense of 'to free from blame.'

P. 64, l. 4. **at every exigency**, whenever you are in need of money.

l. 9. **a treasury extent**, if an individual owes money to the Crown, a treasury extent may be issued, that is, his lands may be valued for the recovery of the debt. But if the whole colony owes a debt, whose lands are to be taken ?

l. 10. **new restraining laws,** referring to Lord North's Fisheries bill.

l. 11. **new acts,** etc.   See on p. 55, l. 3.

l. 14. **An intestine fire,** etc.   There will always be the danger of an outburst in America, just as there is always a danger of an eruption of a volcano.   The language is perhaps a reminiscence of Milton's "combustible and fuelled entrails conceiving fire" of Ætna (*P. L.* i. 232).

l. 21. **standing,** constant.

l. 24. **breaking the union,** on the Roman principle of ruling by creating divisions amongst the ruled.   If the colonies could only be engaged in a quarrel with one another as to the fairness of their respective contributions, there would be no chance of their uniting against England.

l. 27. **to their taste,** palatable to them.

l. 28. **I will not suspect,** etc., a Minister must have some object in view when he introduces a measure into Parliament. As Lord North could not have expected to raise revenue, he must have hoped to produce discord.

P. 65, l. 3. **for certain colonies only,** namely, for those who elected to contribute in lieu of being taxed.

l. 5. **contingent,** not certain.

l. 9. **to whose influence,** etc.   Cf. p. 5, l. 30.

l. 10. **win every inch,** the metaphor is from a general fighting his way through a hostile country.

l. 15. **I mean to spare it,** I have no further arguments by which I could hope to convince you.

l. 23. **No !** an expression of surprise that such a statement should be made.

l. 24. **of Refusal,** of giving or not giving as he pleases.   Grants are large in proportion as they are given willingly.   "Among the many excellent parts of this speech, I find you have got many proselytes by so cleverly showing that the way to get most revenue is to let it come freely from them.   This removes the only possible or plausible ground our adversaries had" (Duke of Richmond, Letter to Burke, June 16, 1775).

l. 28. **It does not indeed,** etc., Burke goes into farthings to emphasize the pettiness of the views of his opponents.

l. 30. **it gives,** etc., loyal subjects will put the whole of their revenues at your disposal.

l. 31. **from whence only,** only men with the instincts of slaves will submit to have their money taken from them against their will.

l. 32. **Posita luditur arca,** Juvenal, *Sat.* i. 90, describing the gambling prevalent in Rome, says that when men sat down to play they risked their strong-box, that is, their whole fortune, on the game. Just as a gambler had the chance of winning the whole fortune of his opponent, so England might look forward to winning the whole wealth of America. Burke is fond of metaphors drawn from the card table ; cf. p. 4, l. 27.

l. 33. **at this time of day,** with all your experience.

l. 34. **a House of Commons,** the House of Commons, which was never obliged to employ force to raise revenue, and only contributed what it pleased to the Crown, ought to be the last body in the world to doubt the productiveness of the voluntary system.

l. 35. **accumulated a debt,** men of business would not have lent this amount to government unless they had felt sure that money would be voted for the repayment of the debt.

P. 66, l. 5. **its trust,** see note on p. 3, l. 10 : **Such a presumption,** etc., he who suspects one government must suspect all governments.

l. 7. **penury of supply,** deficient revenue.

l. 8. **in nature,** so long as men are what they are, governments will not want money, for the reason given in the following sentence.

l. 12. **the stock,** the accumulated wealth. We use the word *capital.* The word *stock* will be familiar to readers of Adam Smith. When property is not safe there can be no motive for accumulating it.

l. 17. **could be squeezed,** etc., let governments apply as much pressure as they please, they can get nothing from them that have nothing. The *husk* is the dry shell from which the grain has been extracted : **politic,** political.

l. 24. **holds the balance of the state,** has supreme power in his hands. Burke means that all parties will be anxious to conciliate the government, because it is only through the government that they can secure the ends which they are anxious to realize. **The parties,** etc., gamblers sit round a table, and each stakes a certain amount of money upon a given result. If the result is other than that on which a man bets, his stake is forfeited to the proprietor of the gambling house—the man who keeps the table. On the other hand, if a gambler wins, he receives so many times his stake from the proprietor. Political parties are compared by Burke to the players. Just as a player can only receive the profits for which he plays from the keeper of the table, so parties can only get their measures carried through the government.

l. 31. **Ease would retract,** etc., Milton, *P. L.* iv. 96. Burke has substituted *retract* for *recant.* A man may, when in difficulties, make a promise; but when the difficulties are over, he will refuse to be bound by it, on the ground that it was made under constraint.

l. 33. **compounding,** see on p. 63, l. 4.

l. 34. **poor,** contemptible.

l. 36. **so may I speed,** etc., a forcible mode of expressing his sincerity—'if I do not think so, I pray that I may fail in my object.'

P. 67, l. 10. **in loan,** in the form of a loan.

l. 11. **if ever,** etc., the country was rich; the people were weak and unwarlike: the company was absolute and unscrupulous.

l. 15. **If America,** etc. Goods were imported from America into England to be re-exported for sale in other countries. The profits of the foreign sales exceeded the amount of the customs duties paid on importation.

l. 23. **with the enemies,** etc., viz., the French and the Spaniards, who had settlements in America as well as England.

l. 32. **light as air,**

> "Trifles *light as air*
> Are to the jealous confirmation strong
> As proofs of Holy Writ" (*Othello*, iii. 3. 332).

links of iron, *Jul. Cæsar*, i. 3. 94.

l. 35. **grapple to you,** cling close to you.

> "Those friends thou hast, and their adoption tried,
> *Grapple* them to thy soul with hoops of steel"
> (*Hamlet*, i. 3. 62).

under heaven, a common Biblical expression.

l. 36. **let it be once understood,** etc., if they are once convinced that they cannot be subject to England without losing rights and privileges, they will revolt from you.

P. 68, l. 3. **the cement,** a favourite metaphor with Burke. He employs it again in his *Reflections on the Revolution in France.*

l. 6. **the sanctuary of liberty,** literally, a place in which liberty is safe—in which it would be sacrilege to violate it.

l. 7. **our common faith,** the worship of freedom. Englishmen all over the world will respect the authority of England so long as subjection to that authority means freedom.

l. 8. **the chosen race,** the privileged race. The expression is commonly applied to the Jews, who regarded themselves as a race specially favoured by God. "For thou art an holy people unto the Lord thy God: the Lord thy God hath chosen thee to be a special people unto himself, above all people that are upon the face of the earth " (*Deut.* vii. 6).

l. 9. **turn their faces towards you,** Perhaps a reminiscence of *Daniel*, vi. 10, "Daniel went into his house ; and his windows being open in his chamber towards Jerusalem, he kneeled upon his knees three times a day, and prayed, and gave thanks before his God "; and, ix. 3, "And I set my face unto the Lord God, to seek by prayer and supplication," etc. Cf. also *ibid.* 11, 17, 18, 19.

l. 15. **natural dignity,** not only do you gain by treating the Americans as free men, because they contribute more liberally if allowed to contribute freely, but it is unworthy of you to treat men of your own race as slaves.

l. 17. **of which you have the monopoly,** which they can buy from you only. **This is the true act,** etc. Burke means to say that the Americans only allow themselves to be bound by the Act of Navigation, because they love the power which imposes the act.

l. 19. **the wealth of the world,** etc., because the act gave to England the profits of the carrying trade, and also because England made large profits by the resale of those commodities which the colonies might export to England alone.

l. 22. **weak an imagination,** foolish an idea.

l. 23. **your registers,** etc., *i.e.* the regulations of your custom-houses : **affidavits,** declarations on oath.

l. 24. **sufferances,** permits : **cockets,** the sealed document delivered as evidence that the proper dues had been paid on goods. The word means, literally, the custom-house seal : **clearances,** the technical word for passing goods through the custom-house.

l. 26. **letters of office,** official letters written by English Ministers : **instructions,** sent by the English government to the colonial governors.

l. 28. **the mysterious whole,** perhaps a reminiscence of Pope's *Essay on Man*,

" All are but parts of one stupendous whole,
    Whose body nature is and God the soul."

These things do not make, etc. Cf. " Mr. Grenville conceived, and many conceived along with him, that the flourishing trade of this country was greatly owing to law and institution, and not quite so much to liberty : for but too many are apt to believe regulations to be commerce, and taxes to be revenue" (Burke, *On American Taxation*).

l. 32. **infused through the mighty mass,** The phraseology is suggested by a passage in Vergil, " The whole world is nourished by a spirit within it, and soul, diffused throughout its parts, animates the whole mass."

P. 69, l. 3. **the mutiny bill,** which enables the offences of soldiers to be tried by military law. The Mutiny Bill is passed afresh every year, and the money required for the support of the army is also voted every year. The object of this is to make the very existence of an army depend on the consent of Parliament. If the Sovereign maintained or controlled the army, he might employ it against the Parliament or the people.

l. 6. **the deep stake,** etc., how much they would lose if the government were altered or overthrown. The metaphor is a very common one. For the literal meaning of *stake* see on p. 59, l. 28.

l. 8. **liberal,** worthy of freemen, opposed to servile. Burke means obedience rendered from love, not from fear. Cf. *Reflections on the Revolution in France.*

l. 10. **chimerical,** fanciful, literally, as unreal as the *chimœra,* a fabulous monster of the old Greek mythology.

l. 11. **the profane herd,** borrowed from Horace, *Od.* iii. 1. 1 : **mechanical,** because they think that everything can be effected by the machinery of political regulations, and allow nothing for the spontaneous action of human will and feeling.

l. 12. **no place,** no right to a place.

l. 13. **gross and material,** as opposed to what is *spiritual,* viz., man's ideas and feelings. With the whole of this passage, cf. " Nations are not primarily ruled by laws ; less by violence. Whatever original energy may be supposed either in force or regulation, the operation of both is, in truth, merely instrumental. Nations are governed by the same methods and on the same principles by which an individual without authority is often able to govern those who are his equals or superiors ; by a knowledge of their temper and a judicious management of it " (*Present Discontents*).

l. 19. **all in all,** "that God may be *all in all*" (1 *Cor.* xv. 28).

l. 23. **to auspicate,** to begin. The word implies that if we do not so begin, we cannot hope to succeed. For the meaning of the word, see on p. 12, l. 35.

l. 25. **Lift up your hearts,** In the English Church service this is addressed by the priest to the people, and the people reply, "We lift them up unto the Lord." Just as in an act of worship we should lift our thoughts from earth to heaven, so in the business of government we should endeavour to rise above all mean and petty considerations to high ideas and worthy aims.

l. 26. **that trust,** that power which is to be used for the benefit of those over whom it is exercised, just as the money of a minor is to be administered by the guardian for the benefit of his ward

l. 28. **this high calling,** "I press toward the mark for the prize of *the high calling* of God in Christ Jesus" (*Ep. Philipp.* iii. 13).

P. 70, l. 1. **and may it,** etc., words of good omen.

l. 2. **lay the first stone,** for the metaphor, cf. p. 47, l. 8.

l. 9. **the previous question,** viz., whether Burke's motion should be put to the vote at all. It was decided by a majority of a hundred and ninety-two that it should not.

INDEX TO THE NOTES.

PRINTED IN GREAT BRITAIN BY ROBERT MACLEHOSE AND CO. LTD
THE UNIVERSITY PRESS, GLASGOW